MARTIN BELL
COMPLETE POEMS

MARTIN BELL

COMPLETE POEMS

EDITED BY PETER PORTER

BLOODAXE BOOKS

First published 1988 by
Bloodaxe Books Ltd,
Eastburn,
South Park,
Hexham,
Northumberland NE46 1BS.

www.bloodaxebooks.com

For further information about Bloodaxe titles
please visit our website and join our mailing list
or write to the above address for a catalogue.

Supported using public funding by
**ARTS COUNCIL
ENGLAND**

The poems from page 31 to page 131 inclusive are
reprinted from Martin Bell's *Collected Poems 1937-1966*
(Macmillan, 1967)

Frontispiece etching by George Szirtes.

Typesetting by Bryan Williamson, Manchester.

Digital reprint of the 1988 Bloodaxe Books edition.

Contents

MARTIN BELL

A wartime portrait taken in the Middle East

Introduction, Memoir and Critical Note

When Martin Bell died in Leeds in the winter of 1978, he had just turned sixty years of age. He was far less well-known as a poet than he deserved to be. This claim is made regularly for writers once celebrated and thereafter neglected, when their works are reintroduced to the public. With Bell, it is nothing more than the plain truth. Martin Bell is one of the major poets writing in English in the second half of the century, and the fact that his work has been largely unobtainable since his death (and fugitive even in his lifetime) makes the issue of this *Complete Poems* an important and timely event.

Bell's publishing history is singular. His first book was also his *Collected Poems* and his last publication. His precocity as a poet suffered an early frost due both to war service and to personal circumstances, so that his flowering came in early middle age – especially in the decade 1955 to 1965. He was one of the three poets included in volume three of the newly-established series *Penguin Modern Poets* in 1962 (the others were George Barker and Charles Causley). The poems in this Penguin formed the basis of his hardback *Collected* (Macmillan, 1967). The hundred-odd pages of this book are a brilliant distillation of his talent, and, until his death, comprised his life's work on view. He published nothing further, other than to contribute occasional poems to magazines and journals. Several of his enterprises for publishers, during his years living in Leeds, included poems, though none of these larger designs was brought to a successful conclusion.

Many poems were written and given to friends, and much other material was left among his papers at his death. The greater part of his legacy to posterity from this period is contained in his translations of French poets of the Surrealist epoch, which I refer to later in this introduction. Nevertheless I have had a considerable mass of poetry to go through in order to compile what I feel may justifiably be called the *Complete Poems*. Complete here means everything of Bell's which is original poetry, and not translation, prose exegesis, memoir or diary.

The book inevitably falls into two parts. The first consists of the 1967 *Collected* which I have reproduced unaltered, other than to place four pieces of Juvenilia at the front instead of assigning them to the end, as made sense originally. It seemed to me unquestionable that a book which Bell himself prepared for the press must be made the heart of this new enterprise, a conviction sharpened by the high quality of almost everything he had chosen in 1967.

The second part of the book is inevitably my choice of the poems which, as Bell's literary executor, I received from his heirs and friends. I had one crucial decision to make right at the start. Was I to include at least a sample of Bell's copious and brilliant work at translating from the French – say his versions of Rimbaud's *Les Illuminations*, those most difficult to render marvels of proto-modernism (nobody has done 'Départ' as well as he has)? After all, his own 1967 selection included his version of Nerval's 'El Desdi-chado', his Laforgue fantasy 'Winter Coming On' and an even more direct translation from Corbière, 'The Ballad Singer at the Pardon of St Anne'. But in that volume the balance was exact: translations were set against the power of original poems and thus could be seen to carry the full weight of the poet's own personal style, however well they achieved the intention of the original French. The mass of post-1967 poems with which I was dealing was more disparate and was outnumbered threefold by the quantity of translated poetry I had to choose from. I decided, therefore, to leave out any poems which originated in other men's and women's imaginations. Such a decision does not exclude from this book, however, all trace of the presiding preoccupation of his last decade: poems, wholly his own, pay tribute to Benjamin Péret, Pierre Reverdy and Max Jacob, and the shapes and forms of much of his later verse reflects the manner of the French Surrealists.

One further area of the Bell archive worried me. Joan Russell, one of his circle of friends in Southampton before the war and a regular correspondent of Martin's during the hostilities, sent me samples of the poetry he composed while in the forces. Martin Bell had decided when choosing for his *Collected Poems* to ignore all this material, perhaps because he had preserved little of it. Instead, he represented his early years by merely four pieces of Juvenilia, where the Surrealist influence is already recognisable. Mrs Russell con-firmed that she and her surviving friends of the Southampton circle did not possess more than a part of the work which Bell sent home to Southampton from camps in England and the Mediterranean. The passages which she sent me decided me to imitate the poet's example and not collect any of this verse here. What I have read is characteristic and touching but organised at a much less concise and powerful level than anything which Bell chose to print in his mature years. It is heavily reliant on parody and is quite derivative: nor did I ever hear him refer to his poetic output during the war. Had more of his poetry of this period survived, I might have made a different decision.

Martin Bell's life can be seen all too easily as a cautionary tale of the price the poet pays for inspiration. Indeed, it is already being represented this way in some quarters. It is no secret that his later years were blighted by addiction to alcohol, and complicated by depression, lack of recognition, shortage of money and touches of paranoia. It is quite easy, of course, to accept this pattern and still go on to praise Bell as a poet – indeed, if one wants to achieve the full romantic apotheosis, the life's agony is a necessary pre-condition of the ultimate vindication. That Bell deserves wholehearted vindication for a life almost religiously devoted to poetry is beyond doubt, yet such an approach to him and to his verse is both a simplification and a misrepresentation. All who knew him well will assert that he remained at all times, to use an appellation which Auden was fond of, 'no wet-leg'.

He was a man of great charm, enormous erudition and, despite his devotion to serious literature, someone who observed the world around him with extra-journalistic sharpness and wit. The hermetic poet in him shared a sensibility with the worldly moralist and social critic. He was the true inheritor of the Auden mantle (his only rival the slightly older Gavin Ewart), and, even during his later concentration on twentieth-century French poetry, he kept faith with the thirties' creed of poetry as an agent of moral healing, a tracking down of the spoor of history as it is imprinted on our world. He had a highly developed sense of the poet as magus, refiner of the tribal language and high priest of psychic understanding. Sometimes it seemed paradoxical, in his later years, to find him, broke and slightly bewildered, speaking of the poet's power and pride which made him a dangerous adversary and forceful catalyst. Music and Jungian concepts were the only orders which came near to sharing the supremacy of poetry in his imagination once his disillusion with the Communist Party took him out of active politics.

In one of his best poems, 'Reasons for Refusal', Bell invokes his friend Roger Frampton, 'desert-killed in '40', as 'a pattern of accomplishments...joined the Party first, and left it first'. These words can be used of Bell himself if the accomplishments be taken further to include infallible taste in literature and moral generosity. Nor did he ever desert the idealism which possessed so many of the finer spirits of his generation: he was always a man of the Left, even if he loved to add a Gidean '*hélas*' after claiming to be so. He was prescient of the dreadful blight of right-wing reaction in which we find ourselves today, recording as early as 1961 the way things were going in an England bored with the egalitarianism and libertarianism of the post-war Labour governments

> We didn't want to say the way things went
> Pissed on the hopes we entertained,
> Naïve, of course, but vivid and still pissed on –
> The old gang born again in young careerists –
> (Christ, boy, they're reading *The Times* now!)

What he would have made of Thatcher's Britain I cannot imagine. My feelings vary between relief that he is out of it and regret that the philippics it would have spurred him to will never be written. We have many pre-echoes, however, in his poetry of twenty years earlier – 'But the terrifying thing/ Is houses,/ A stake in the country ....Something to hand down....Dismal boxes voting tory.'

Martin Bell was born in Southampton in 1918 and lived there until he was twenty-one. His father worked for the Southern Railway, and Bell always described his parents as lower middle-class. Certainly, there was not much money about during his childhood and manhood, and this prevented his profiting from his education to enable him to set out on a literary career – at least until he was in his thirties. The war, of course, was a further obstruction to his progress. But it was not poverty which rankled with him so consistently, but the fearful gentility which went with it. Poem after poem testifies to the warping influence of lower middle-class respectability, most clearly felt in people's sexual lives. Only D.J. Enright, in *The Terrible Shears* ('Whatever sex was, it was another enemy') has covered this ground as effectively: the novelist's world of keeping up appearances, sexual timidity and class embarrassment has never much appealed to poets, and only Bell and Enright have made it eloquent as verse. His relationship with his mother was close and neurasthenic, as late memoirs, letters and a dream-diary indicate. One of his most sardonic poems is called 'Ode to Psychoanalysis' and it indicates clearly that this expensive therapy could not lift the weight of childhood neurosis from his mind. But Bell was always able to place them in a larger context where the personal becomes the general. His perfect command of rhetoric never deserted him. The 'Ode to Psychoanalysis' ends with him 'suffering Hell because I'm always overdrawn/ At the bank whose manager hovers/ Clacking revengeful shears// Hey there! Nobodaddy!/ That's *my* flaming sword...' The Blake reference is not just a neat summing up, it ties in with all the invocations to penis, bowels and negative transference, and reminds us that Freudianism is based in prophetic religion as strongly as in medical science.

14

Bell was 'a scholarship boy' at Taunton's School, Southampton from 1928 till 1935, and then took an external London Honours Degree in English at University College, Southampton (now Southampton University) in 1938, and a Cambridge Diploma of Education in 1939. Again, he held a scholarship. It was clear to all who met him in these years that Bell was a brilliant scholar, but he was also not a conformist and he attracted as much hostility as support from his superiors. In fact, the Principal of University College considered him a misfit (no games, not even any bird-watching or brass-rubbing, but an interest in French Symbolist poetry) and a ring-leader of the subversive element among the students. The opposition he aroused prevented his being recommended for academic posts, just as his parents' poverty caused his headmaster at Taunton's to advise against trying for Cambridge.

Despite all this, Bell's pre-war career was not undistinguished. Two of his teachers, Vivian de Sola Pinto and J.B. Leishman, were distinguished men of letters, the first being a pioneer editor of the Earl of Rochester and the second the best-known translator (with Stephen Spender) of Rilke's *Duino Elegies*. There was never anything provincial about Bell's attitude to literature, and however hard he fought the class war he was not intimidated in the slightest by literati from the public schools and ancient universities. He knew he had read more than they had, and he knew he could write better. The paradox of his early years is his combination of confidence in his own powers (far greater than that of most budding poets) and an accompanying diffidence of expression. It was shortage of money, pressure of family and the onset of war which cauterised his career. By the time he began to bring his poetry to fruition, he was no longer a young man. Men of his own generation had pushed ahead, and it was left to those ten or more years younger to become his colleagues.

His allegiance to the Communist Party was the talisman of those years in Southampton. It was also the centre around which his network of friends revolved. Many years later, in his *Collected Poems*, he wrote a threnody for David Guest, one of the Southampton lecturers and a leading party member, killed in the Spanish War fighting the Fascists. Bell and his friends took Communism seriously, both for its doctrine and for its strategic directives. In an extended curriculum vitae, compiled as late as 1977, he describes why he volunteered for the army in October 1939. 'At the beginning of the war I made up my mind I was going to survive it, and told people so. I was not the type to make a military hero: in cold blood I was cowardly, I was physically clumsy, hopeless at games and PT,

15

had a slightly deformed foot which stopped me marching in step, and bad eye-sight. I would, out of my conviction at that time, have been a conscientious objector, but the party line forbade that. In order to avoid being called up into the infantry, I volunteered for the Royal Engineers.'

The party line was something they all took seriously, and although the Ribbentrop/Molotov pact was signed in these months, most Communist supporters, including Bell, did not leave the party until the full horror of Stalinism was revealed in the immediate post-war period. Bell, like so many others, began his disillusionment by reading Koestler's *Darkness at Noon*. The Party makes several appearances in his poems – as the true faith betrayed, as a sort of parallel to the Catholic Summa, abandoned but not forgotten ('the Party Line'), and as a substitute for the gorgon images of Freudian theory. 'Ode to Psychoanalysis' shows Bell coming to terms with two father-figures, Marx and Freud.

> So the analysis was cut off
> After I hadn't paid him
> For over two months –
> He took two-fifths of my wages.
> ...
>
> I still wanted to kill Stalin
> After that. But I felt I'd let Freud down.
> The cook would not run the State,
> And the State wouldn't wither away,
> And psychoanalysis
> Was very expensive indeed:
> Postpone, for the time being,
> The New Jerusalem.

Joan Russell's memories of their Southampton circle identify Martin as the inspiration of a whole Hampshire generation launched into higher education at the end of the Depression. Though he wrote regularly to many of these friends during his six and a quarter years in the forces, he did not return to Southampton when the war ended, preferring to take up teaching in London. Southampton seems almost to have dropped out of his life, coming back only in brief appearances in poems (the fine 'High Street, Southampton', with its memorable comment on the blitzing of the town centre, restored in so ugly a fashion – 'Where is the Phoenix? Surely there was burning'). Marriage was another cause of distancing. He acquired a completely new set of friends and colleagues, very much London-based. The fact that he preserved none of the poems he

sent in letters to Southampton points to a resolve, however uncon-
scious, to make a new start in life. But his early leadership was
prescient of what happened later. With the Group, he found a new
circle in which his talent could prosper, and this time he was tooled-
up to take full advantage of it.

Martin's wartime experience was formative in another way. It
freed him from English provincialism. He served in Lebanon, Syria
and Italy mainly. His war was like so many bookish persons' wars,
mostly boredom in camp and apparently pointless enterprises
abroad. But he relished the chance to speak French and to attend
the opera in Italy (San Carlo Opera House, in Naples, where he
was introduced to the basic Italian operatic repertory, and where he
first saw and heard Tito Gobbi). Opera was to remain for him the
art closest to poetry in its combination of humanism and irrational
emotion. There were other aspects of army life which he appreci-
ated: the 1977 c.v. has a remarkable tribute to the Royal Engineers.
'In the unit with which I served longest, the whole company, from
the OC and Adjutant (who kept sometimes ignorant junior officers
in order), through the Sergeant Major and NCOs (I was a lance-
corporal), to the Sappers and Drivers, all *conspired* to keep the Com-
pany's good name in spite of its short-comings, lied for each other,
and kept one another out of trouble.'

The same devotion to a team characterised Martin Bell's relations
with those of us later who formed the Group. He enjoyed the con-
spiratorial mode of rivalry in the world of poetry, and once he had
made his reputation, he never departed from a concern for the
republic of letters. In this, his highmindedness was out of tune with
the increasing fashion-consciousness of the sixties and seventies
and led him into many disappointments. He could not understand
that many of the well-known poets of his time were ruthless egotists
who had little interest in promoting anyone but themselves. The
pro bono publico aspect of his nature made him a wonderful teacher
of poetry, if his student was talented and genuine. He can claim to
have discovered one of today's leading poets, George Szirtes, who
was an art student in Leeds while Martin taught Liberal Studies
there and whom he encouraged to write verse. Many other students
in Leeds learned how wide and diverse European poetry is from Bell.

Bell ran a sawmill in Lebanon and polished up his French there.
The first poem in his *Collected* comes from his time in Italy, and it
is a translation from Nerval's French, 'El Desdichado', the sonnet
which T.S. Eliot gave wider immortality to by quoting from it prom-
inently at the end of *The Waste Land*. Bell's version is not only far

and away the best that has been done, but it launches his published poems on a virtuoso note. Because he is essentially a realistic and vernacular writer, it is important to underline his virtuosity. His style is a yoking of salient detail to rhetorical projection. To achieve this, the poet needs to be a master of phrasing, syntax and drama: from 'El Desdichado' onwards, his verse is never afraid to be flamboyant, but always stays close to the spoken word. His erudition is so natural that the many references and quotations in his poetry (a tendency both natural to him and imitated from Eliot, who was his ideal model all his life) dovetail into the pattern neatly. The opposite of the 'know-nothing' poet, Bell nevertheless has little of the cold academicism of many educated and 'serious' poets. He is closer to Wallace Stevens, who felt simple emotions voluptuously, and a similar fondness for 'essential gaudiness' informs Bell's verse. However straightforward and lean, it is always rhetorical.

He settled in London after the war, married and had two daughters. His first appointment as a teacher with the LCC was in a junior school whose headmaster he found sympathetic. He worked as a teacher there for ten years. This part of his life is the least well-documented, since Martin rarely spoke of it. It was clearly a period of calm and consolidation in his career. The very decade itself was a time of hope but also a time of austerity, as the post-war governments called on the nation to make sacrifices to build the new and hopeful Britain promised by the Labour Party. He must have read a great deal and begun to write again.

Clearly, there had been troubles. Soon after demobilisation he entered psychoanalysis, which was not a success. He tells how he wrote limericks against his analyst who, while attributing them to aggression, went on to encourage him by saying something could be made of them. Bell, however, had been apologising for their imperfections, and not for having written them, and angrily told his analyst that he knew the precise weight of words and could tell a good limerick from a bad one. The upshot was uncomfortable: he appreciated that the last thing he consciously wanted the analyst to find out was that he thought of himself as a poet. It would not be going too far to suggest that he had no further need of analysis once he had accepted his calling to poetry. It was to bring him close to destitution, but it also liberated him from suburban despair.

At the beginning of the fifties, he was writing poetry again, though not yet regularly. The second poem in his *Collected*, 'Benefit Night at the Opera' was accepted by J.R. Ackerley for *The Listener*. Bell recalls that he had worked for three years on its twenty lines. It is his first characteristic poem, being an amalgam of several actual operas, most notably *Un Ballo in Maschera*, plus memories of evenings spent in the San Carlo house, all worked into a menacing mise-en-scène in Auden's manner.

A few years later, he went into his usual pub in Chiswick where an encounter with a young man changed his life. He was reading quietly when a youthful gentleman with a cultivated and resonant voice approached him and said: 'Excuse me, sir, but does that happen to be a volume of verse you are reading?' 'It is indeed, sir.' 'May I enquire what it is? Surely it is Norman Cameron's translation of Rimbaud's verse-poems.'

The young interrogator was Peter Redgrove, also living then at Chiswick, who immediately invited Bell to come to the newly-convened meetings of aspirant poets which were being held in Philip Hobsbaum's flat. This conventicle had been founded by Hobsbaum in Cambridge at the same time that Redgrove, an undergraduate who had turned from Natural Sciences to English, founded the magazine *Delta*. Hobsbaum continued these sessions in London and thus the Group, as it came to be called, began its ten-year life. Hobsbaum was the first chairman and may be called the Group's 'onlie begetter'. Early members included Redgrove, Edward Lucie-Smith, Alan Brownjohn, Margaret Owen, Martin Bell, George Mac-Beth and myself.

From the very first evening he attended, Bell became the father and tone-setter of Group discussions. He had read more than any of us; was, of course, older, but was also more audacious, intellectually wide-ranging and freer from prejudice. This is not the place to explain the Group's principles, other than to state that Hobsbaum's rule was that we should look for everything we wanted to say in the text itself, and that the person whose work was being discussed was not allowed to intervene in the discussion with explanations of his or her intentions. My memories of Martin at Group sessions are vivid: he would begin with a cough of emphatic intervention and immediately develop brilliant technical fantasies on the roneo'd text which left the rest of us labouring behind. He was also a fine delineator of versification and verbal troping. He loved the camaraderie of discussion, the sense that, like any of those involved in the peripateia of the past, we were pioneers of creativity and understanding.

I doubt that Martin learned from us, his juniors, much in the way of useful knowledge for his work, but he gained confidence in his audience, and, encouraged by more worldly figures, he began to send out poems. Soon after joining the Group, he read a poem, 'The Enormous Comics' at one of G.S. Fraser's meetings in Beaufort Street, and George Fraser took it for the *TLS*. In the period between 1955, when he began to come to Group meetings, and 1962, Bell wrote most of his first wave of poems, and saw them published, sporadically but with mounting success, in various journals. Group members began to make their first excursions into book publication as the decade ended. First was Peter Redgrove, whose debut was in 1960, with *The Collector*. Edward Lucie-Smith and I followed in 1961, and George MacBeth soon after. When my poems were accepted for the launching of *Penguin Modern Poets* (publication early 1962), Bell's were already being considered for the series in Penguin's offices. His inclusion in Number Three of the series came later the same year. Martin Bell was now securely on the Poetry Scene.

I am grateful to the Group for all that it did, and especially for its liberating insistence that poetry was not so arcane an art that it could not be discussed helpfully. And I remember Martin as the epicentre of Group activity. Nevertheless, my strongest and fondest memories of him come from outside Group meetings, though still within the ambience of literature. He was a marvellous talker, ranging in all directions and into hundreds of special regions. He and I loved Auden and the thirties, while Group orthodoxy, influenced by Leavis, was suspicious of that decade and its poets. Martin and I were less than enchanted with Lawrence, another aberration by Group standards.

Music was a further affection, and here I was unable to extend Martin's love of opera into an accompanying enjoyment of instrumental music. We also deviated in our opinion of Britten's operas, Martin having an unswerving dislike of *Billy Budd*, for its sadomasochism and homosexuality, which he later passionately argued with Anthony Burgess. This analysis of Britten also informed his views of Wilfred Owen's poetry, so that when the *War Requiem* was performed, it was loaded with a double helping of obloquy. Stravinsky's collaboration with Auden was a different matter and his affection and understanding of *The Rake's Progress* was intense. He also esteemed *Der Rosenkavalier* and Mozart's operas. His greatest love was reserved for Verdi, and several of his poems pay tribute to this most manly and accessible of composers.

Martin and his wife and my wife and I exchanged visits many times in the sixties, until Martin's marriage broke up. He and I also did poetry readings, travelled over England and, all in all, saw a great deal of each other in this, his high noon as a poet. I owe him more than I could ever repay for his kindnesses and understandings, and for his sheer human warmth.

My memories of Bell in his heyday would not be complete without some recall of the extraordinary partnership he made with Peter Redgrove. I have never met two people with a greater knowledge and relish of poetry in English. Their fondness was almost a musical one, in that it was the sounds of English verse which excited them – not sounds in any Sitwellian sense, that would be too limiting. Rather, it was a love of the way syntax, meaning, resonance and recall are all woven into the greatest English poetry. Sitting in the Mandrake Club one dark afternoon, I heard Redgrove and Bell give an inspired duo performance of Wallace Stevens's 'Sea Surface Full of Clouds'. The different tones of their voices as they dealt in turn with Stevens's refrain 'In that November off Tehuantepec/ The slopping of the sea grew still...' was a revelation to me, always someone more moved by the phrasing of poetry than by its sound, and their concern for the dramatic poise of poetry approached sacerdotal intensity.

In more uproarious mood, they would give a performance of *Macbeth* in cod Scottish accents, which were hardly more ridiculous than Orson Welles's voice in his film. It's surprising how well Shakespeare's lines appear to support some kind of accentual Doric – viz. 'The air hath bubbles as the water hath.' One of the regular pieces in their double act was a performance of Redgrove's dialogue poem 'The Play', a rather Beckettian piece in which two old gentlemen outbid each other in fustian and second-childhood-fantasy. When taking part in this, Martin's residual Hampshire accent would swell to high camp Mummerset, and his intoning of the final couplet was worthy of his idol Groucho Marx:

Is that my part? Now watch my art
As I die as I scream as I die for my art.

The serious aspect of Bell's generosity in these remarkable years, as the fifties changed to the sixties, was his own poetry, which came from him in an undiverted stream. Always a careful and revising writer, nevertheless he produced poem after poem with splendid facility. At Group meetings, we encountered many examples of vintage Bell: 'Headmaster: Modern Style', 'Reasons for Refusal', 'Winter Coming On', 'Ode to Himself', 'High Street, Southampton', 'Ode to Groucho' and 'Letter to a Friend'.

With 'Techniques for Détente', 'Zen for William Empson' and 'Verdi at Eighty' we approach the last stage of Martin's London period. His fantasias of an old man, whereby he invented for himself the persona of Don Senilio, show his imagination modulating out of the essentially happy years of his discovery of the Group towards the alienation and disorientation of the Seventies. When Don Senilio was conceived, Bell was hardly more than forty-five years old, but the character of a man washed up on the shoals of redundancy came to him with the sharpness of a revelation. His life was changing, and not in hopeful directions, despite some initially favourable moves.

In 1964, he was awarded the first Arts Council poetry bursary, which enabled him to work part-time. Then, in 1967, he was appointed Gregory Fellow of Poetry at Leeds University for two years. He abandoned teaching, the job he had laboured at unhappily for almost twenty years. He separated from his wife, a separation felt bitterly by her. His removal to Leeds was to prove final. He never lived in London again, and saw the city only as a visitor. He regarded his life from 1967 onwards as exile.

Martin always believed that if he had remained in London, both success and failure would have been more manageable. There is some reason for agreeing with him. For instance, in the early sixties he formed a close relationship with Anthony Burgess and his first wife, Lyn, then living in Chiswick. Bell and Burgess formed a double-act only slightly less playful than the Bell/Redgrove one. Burgess had him appointed opera critic for *Queen* magazine in 1965, in succession to Burgess himself. Martin was an idiosyncratic critic of music and opera, but, in many respects, a sound and unsnobbish one. His hand lay behind some of Burgess's own judgments, especially of Stravinsky and Britten, though it was Burgess who was the trained musician of the two. Bell was a jaunty figure at the opera, and claimed that the Glyndebourne authorities had waived the requirement of evening dress for him, considering him sufficiently well accoutred wearing a bow-tie to go with the small dapper beard which he affected at this time.

The year 1965 was a crucial one in Martin Bell's life. In 1963, some Group members, including Bell and I, had read on the Fringe at the Edinburgh Festival. On this visit, he met and formed a lively admiration for the Scots poet Robert Garioch. Though not a partisan of Lallans, he always advocated a wider audience for Scottish poetry in England, and once persuaded several of us to put our names to a letter to *The Times* proposing Hugh MacDiarmid, another of the poets we met in Edinburgh, as Poet Laureate in succession to Masefield.

In 1965 poetry was included among the official performances at the Edinburgh Festival for, I believe, the first and only time. A week of readings was organised at the Freemasons' Hall in George Street. Bell and I were again in Edinburgh, hoping to meet Randall Jarrell who was due to arrive from America. Alas, he walked into the freeway a month before. W.D. Snodgrass came in his place, and was welcomed by us enthusiastically. I had been commissioned to interview W.H. Auden for BBC radio. Auden was the star of the Edinburgh series, just as he became later at London's Poetry International. Bell and I spent an evening prowling round Edinburgh desperately trying to think of things I could ask Auden. In the event, the interview was a fiasco, for which I do not blame Auden.

It was an exhilarating time, in and out of the Festival Press Club, drinking with such notables as Vernon Scannell, Hugh MacDiarmid, Sydney Goodsir Smith, and the whole corps of London theatre and music critics. Bell had to write notices of the operas at the King's Theatre (*Don Giovanni* and a rare Haydn work, *Le Pescatrici*, unfortunately very dull), and I remember how thrilled he was to both stand next to Carlo Maria Giulini at the Mayor's reception for the Festival artists and to ask the maestro sympathetic questions at a press conference about the stage mechanics' strike which robbed *Don Giovanni* of all its scenery.

The most important aspect of Edinburgh that year for Martin was his falling in love with Christine McCausland, who became the Muse of his later verse. He returned in the last year of his life to this brief episode of impassioned involvement in a verse-and-prose fantasy left unfinished among his papers. He called it *Operatics and Intrusions*, and the part of it he completed recreates those days at the Edinburgh Festival, on to which he grafts a few new poems and works in some of his best-known previously published verse. From this time on, Bell was determined to change his life, but the Rilkean sense of the phrase came out in tragic guise rather than in life-asserting shape.

His period of office as Gregory Fellow was not a success – at least from his own point of view. He was now cut off from London, and the romance for which he made the break from his previous commitments could not be sustained – chiefly his own responsibility, since he was now drinking very heavily. A year or so previously in London, during the interregnum between his giving up teaching and his removal to Leeds, he had been taken to hospital for an emergency operation for a ruptured duodenal ulcer. He appeared to make a complete recovery from this, but his stomach was now weakened and his health in general began to decline.

After the Gregory, he was taken on as a teacher of Liberal Studies at Leeds Art School, later Leeds Polytechnic. Though he carried out his duties with sporadic brilliance, he began, with the seventies, a long personal decline, coming close to despair on many occasions. I do not intend to describe, even if I could, his life in Leeds. One point needs to be stressed strongly, however. He remained an inspiration to a whole group of people in that city – English and Philosophy teachers, students, painters, aspirant writers – persons of widely varying backgrounds and interests. Nobody talking to Martin for any length of time could miss his originality of mind. And the dislocation of his brain and his body was a tragedy for his body more than for his intellect.

All the while he was lurching from one crisis to another – taking cures for alcoholism, seeking refuge in hospital from bank managers as much as from booze – he was adding methodically to his archive of translations of the French Surrealists. In this work, he was methodical and exemplary – the manuscripts are cleaner and more impeccably set out than almost any I have seen. Of course, such enterprises did nothing to improve his immediate circumstances, financially or in any other way. He was driven to all kinds of resorts to make money.

One undertaking which has left behind a welcome legacy was an expedition to Cyprus in the late sixties with his friend, the painter Stass Paraskos, and Stass's family. From this visit, Martin was commissioned to produce a travel book along the lines of Auden's and MacNeice's, tentatively called *Letters from Cyprus*. The 'letters' which got written were mostly in verse, and I have included most of them in this volume. Bell met and fell completely for President Makarios, but much else on the trip was as nightmarish as anything Rimbaud could have imagined. Bell even hated the France he travelled through. His love was always for the language and literature of that country, not for the people – or the landscape.

Before he died Martin Bell had applied to the Arts Council for a bursary to enable him to complete several projects, including his translations. By the sort of irony common in poets' lives, the money arrived after his death. I met him in London less than four weeks before he died in his sleep, and he seemed more hopeful and relaxed. What surprised most people, in the weeks after his demise, was the scale and scope of work which he left behind him. Nevertheless, it has taken many years to bring this *Complete Poems* into existence. The taste of the times has so far not been encouraging to a poet of Bell's commitments – he would see the point but not admire the

TOP LEFT: *The schoolteacher. A staffroom photograph of Martin Bell taken during the 1950s.*

TOP RIGHT: *In the garden. A picture taken at Grove Park Road, Chiswick, where Martin Bell lived with his family during the early 1960s.*

BOTTOM LEFT: *Martin Bell in Leeds, 1975.*

BOTTOM RIGHT: *Martin Bell in London, Christmas 1977.*

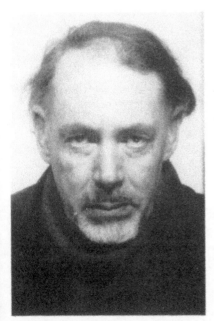

TOP LEFT: *On board ship, en route to Cyprus, summer 1968. Martin Bell with Stass Paraskos (left), Stass's son Stanley, and Christine McCausland.*

TOP RIGHT: *Martin Bell with Christine McCausland and Stass Paraskos's daughter Margaret. Marseille, summer 1968.*

BOTTOM: *Martin Bell and Stass Paraskos meet Archbishop Makarios in the Presidential Palace. Nicosia, summer 1968.*

performance of today's dandies, the Martians, and he would be disappointed at the re-emergence of Oxbridge fashion as the dominating tone of English poetry. A programme on Radio Three which I compiled of his verse in 1983 merely earned censure from the network's cultural officers. But I trust that such neglect is a thing of the past.

I have already outlined the principles on which this collection has been made. All that remains to be done in this introduction is to offer some notes on the poems printed – an editor's justification. Everything up to 'Pets' (page 129) comes from Bell's own *Collected*. I do not feel that any notes are needed. Bell offered none when he first gathered these poems together. The music which Anthony Burgess wrote for 'Senilio's Broadcast Script' has been retained. It presents a challenge to any amateur pianist, with its florid Lisztian bravura. All poems after 'Pets' come from the mass of material in Bell's possession at his death. He had some major enterprises on hand, as well as others which he had abandoned in various states of completion:

1. From *The City of Dreadful Something*

This was to be a sort of mini-*Waste Land*, castigating Leeds and all its works. At various stages, poems were added and deleted. There are other poems, which he did not include in this sequence, which also apostrophise Leeds. I have included them here, after the specific sequence under the above title. The text I have chosen for the sequence appears to be the closest to a definitive one among the many recensions he preserved. The title is parodied from James Thomson's *City of Dreadful Night*.

2. *Letters from Cyprus*

I have given this sequence its title, since Bell's definitive text, clearly gathered from among the many pieces he had intended for the book of that name is, in his final fair copy, unheaded. The sequence is his own, though he obviously intended the book to contain much in the way of prose letters, as Auden's and MacNeice's did, into which these poems would have been leafed. Clearly, he regarded the project as a sort of gallimaufry where many different sorts of poem could be accommodated, even if they had little bearing on Cyprus itself. Thus the sequence includes poems about cats, London life, French poets, Leeds, his old friends, Stass Paraskos's pictures etc. At the end, I have added five further poems which may not be specifically for this undertaking but are connected by subject matter.

3. *Operatics and Intrusions*

I have described this previously, and have taken only two short poems from the text in my possession, the others being works included in *Collected Poems* and here used in a different context.

4. *Translations from French*

Though I have excluded everything in this great mass of material, I shall list what is included under this heading to demonstrate Bell's application to projects which fired his imagination:

MAX JACOB: *Le Cornet à dés*, 226 pages of prose poems.

ANDRÉ BRETON and PHILIPPE SOUPAULT: *Les Champs magnétiques*, 117 pages.

ROBERT DESNOS: *À la mystérieuse*, 24 pages; *Les Ténèbres*, 46 pages.

BENJAMIN PÉRET: *Le Grand Jeu*, A selection.

PIERRE REVERDY: *Poèmes en prose*, 56 pages; *Les jockeys camouflés*, 17 pages; *Étoiles peintes*, 20 pages; *La balle au bond*, 40 pages.

Selections from ARTAUD, BECKER, ÉLUARD, HÉBERT, MESENS and QUENEAU, 70 pages.

There are also versions of Rimbaud, which Bell seems to have thought of as lying outside this specifically twentieth century file.

5. *Diaries*

These are in prose. One is a dream-diary he kept in the last years, in which he interprets his dreams according to Jungian lights. An extensive autobiographical diary also exists. Many letters from him to Peter Redgrove and Christine McCausland have also been pre-served.

In deciding which order to put the post-1967 poetry, I have been, of necessity, somewhat arbitrary. First come his resumptions of the mask character of Don Senilio. Then Leeds is celebrated and execrated, and poems dedicated to Leeds friends are added. Some of the larger shapes among his later works are the next in line, including his addresses to Patricia Highsmith and Bing Crosby. After this, I have placed *Letters from Cyprus* and further poems inspired by the island and the Mediterranean. Now come poems addressed to father-figures and the Frenchmen he translated, together with ruminations on translation. Then some engaging squibs for friends and colleagues in Leeds and elsewhere.

Where Bell did not provide a title, I have, in general, not invented one, so that several poems are listed in the Contents merely by their opening line or lines. This section of the book contains much of the light verse and lampooning which he wrote, including some more savage satires on literary people. Some are fragments. The tone darkens towards the end of the book. Social poems, not satires but denunciations of a crass and materialist society, follow, interspersed with mysterious, almost cryptic laments. Bell's increasing sense of his own mortality emerges in this part.

As far as I have been able to date them, I have kept his final poems to the end. His parents come back in these short verses, as they do in his accounts of his dreams. His love for the lady who was his Muse is faced up to once more. Poem after poem is 'For C' or C's name is worked into its pattern. Their being what he calls defiantly 'love poems' does not prevent his weaving much self-reproach and well-observed pain into them. Almost at the end, dated the year before he died, is his 'A Vocation Possibly' which he sent to Anthony Burgess. It is a quiet poem, but a desolate one.

The great majority of Martin Bell's manuscripts, in long-hand or typed, insist on capitals at the beginning of lines, and I have kept to this preference strictly. His punctuation is a much more open-ended matter. He tended to punctuate in a lordly way, as Byron did. Perhaps both poets expected their editors to put the punctuation in for them. I have done so very gently indeed, so that there are many poems in which punctuation is sparse or non-existent. Meaning, however, is seldom in jeopardy. Lastly, there may be further poems I have not seen. This book reproduces all the original poetry that Martin Bell and his circle kept intact, except for some clearly incomplete and uncompletable pieces.

Amongst the prose Bell left is a brief manifesto which is worth reproducing since its various maxims help a reader not well acquainted with his verse and the thought behind it to understand his procedures, and the strange combination in his nature of sardonic doubt and idealist enthusiasm. He entitled it *Against the Grain: Contradictory Theses.*

> Poetry is too popular. What occurred in the Albert Hall was disaster.
> Poems should be detested, but irresistible.
> 'Doing one's own thing' is as obscene a pun as 'doing one's bit'.
> Crowds are for contracting out of.
> It is necessary to postulate the existence of absolute standards, and to endeavour to approximate to them. These standards are ratios.
> There must be formal etiquette to disinfect applause.
> We are not élitists, but nevertheless have chosen ourselves.
> Enemies: the Don, the Administrator, the Impresario, the Journalist, the Anarchist, and Old Charlie in the corner with the squeeze-box.
> Conspiracy is necessary to Democracy.
> Ancestor-worship is essential. Pope, Baudelaire, pray for us!
> There is no necessity to satirise popular art: this function it performs for itself.

> Some people have not yet heard that Dada is dead!
> The Unconscious should be treated with courtesy, not raped.
> Again and yet again: to purify the dialect of the tribe.
> We are on the Left, hélas!

These admonitions could be taken for reactionary only in a debased age, though they were written at the end of a simple-minded one. Their author knew more about poetry than any writer I have known.

I should like to thank especially the following people for helping to bring this edition of Martin Bell's poems to a successful conclusion – John Milne, Philip Hobsbaum, Alan Brownjohn, George Szirtes, Peter Redgrove, Joan Russell, and, the most essential person of all, without whose devotion to Martin's memory and his legacy of poetry, nothing could have been done – Christine McCausland.

PETER PORTER

COMPLETE POEMS

'Where move the enormous comics, drawn from life...'
W.H. AUDEN

'...there are grounds for the belief that Fields
was dangerously bored by the time he was four.'
ROBERT LEWIS TAYLOR
W.C. Fields

'To know that the balance does not quite rest,
That the mask is strange, however like.'
WALLACE STEVENS

Unfriendly Flowers

Startled, the gardener learns to fear his art –
Seeing spring up, after long, loving hours
Of labour in the garden of his heart,
The vivid, the metallic the unfriendly flowers.

My Blue Heaven

Light hitting you in the eye
Like Sorbo bounced from the asphalt
Light from the pale-blue plaster sky
Light from the glitter of blue water
Flapping full on the shore.

Of course there are paler-trees dotted about all over the place.

The streets are full of friendly faces
And trains dash in and out of the station all day long.

Lecture Notes

let us pass on
        to consider the influence of Anglo-Norman
        to insist that angels and policemen wear black shirts
        jump through the window jump out of the door
        to say, quite suddenly and risen from the dead
        'I, I am Popeye, the Sailor Man'

let us pass on, O, let us pass on
        to the liquidation of Narcissus
        to the decapitation of Father Christmas
        to the final boiling of glass eyes

Prospect 1939
(for Campbell Matthews)

'Life is a journey' said our education,
And so we packed, although we found it slow.
At twenty-one, left stranded at the station
We've heaps of luggage and nowhere to go.

El Desdichado
A gothicised version of Nerval

Look for me in the shadow, a bereft one, disconsolate,
Prince of Aquitaine and heir to a ruined Folly.
One star was mine, gone out now: my starred lute
Goes in dark circuit with the Sun of Melancholy.

O, to console me, in my graveyard midnight,
Bring back Posillipo and Italy's seas,
The flower that was my sad heart's favourite
And friends the rose and vine there, binding trellises.

Am I Eros, then, or Apollo? Lusignan or Byron?
My brow burns red still, which the Queen has kissed.
I have lingered in caverns where the sea-nymphs quire,

And twice, a conqueror, swum the straits of Acheron,
Mingling alternate strains on Orpheus' lyre,
Sighs of the anchorite, wailing of the possessed.

B

A Benefit Night at the Opera

The chatter thins, lights dip, and dusty crimson
Curtains start dragging away. Then, at one bound,
A rush of trumpets, ringing brass and vermilion –
The frescoed nymphs sprawl in a sea of sound.

We give our best attention as we must, for
This music is fatal and must be heard.
The glittering fountains vocalise our lust,
The whole brilliant scene sways on to murder.

The idyll interrupted by a cough,
Coloratura soars into a fever.
After the vows, the sibyl shuffles off,
The conspirators' chorus mutter, melt away, leave us

A traitor and his stabbed tyrant, downstage in tears.
Masked revellers are grouping for a wedding.
In stern beat start to life six scarlet halberdiers,
Move with the music, march to a beheading.

Lo! Wild applause proclaims a happy ending.
Vendetta is achieved with clinking swords.
Sheer from the battlements the Diva is descending,
Rash in black velvet and resplendent chords.

Usumcasane as Poet Maudit

Is it not brave to be a king, Techelles,
Usumcasane, and Theridamas?
Is it not passing brave to be a king
And ride in triumph through Persepolis?

Noses in books, odd children in good schools
Get praise by being clever. And they sing
Revenge on the fortunate, the easy-going fools;
And think it passing brave to be a king.

King then, but of words only. There's the rub.
Action is suspect and its end uncertain:
Stuck in a job, or browned off in a pub,
Or fêted and then stabbed, behind a Curtain...

Impatiently they strain their eyes
To see small faults through powerful lenses:
Angrily snatch at paradise,
Exacerbating their five senses.

Famous young Rimbaud managed rather better –
Crammed all he could beneath his greedy hide,
Went to Abyssinia, wouldn't write a letter:
Was made into a saint before he died.

The Enormous Comics
A Teacher to his Old School

Barnacled, in tattered pomp, go down
Still firing, battered admirals, still go down
With jutting jaw and tutting tooth and tongue,
Commanding order down cold corridors.

Superbly, O dyspeptic Hamlets,
Pause in the doorway, startle the Fourth Form
With rustlings of impatient inky cloaks –
Time and time again you go into your act.

Benevolent and shaven, county cricketers,
Heroes on fag-cards, lolling out of the frame,
Or smug and bun-faced, Happy Families,
Or swollen in shrill rage (Off With His Head!),

You lean huge areas into close-up
With cruel pampered lips like Edward G.
Robinson, or Tracy's anguished eyes,
And still remain the seediest of grandees.

Processioned hierarchically, larger than life,
Gigantic Guy Fawkes masks, great heads on stilts –
Your business was traditional, strictly articulated
Into timetables, only a few steps

From nightmare. Wild clowns will terrify
Wagging a wooden phallus at the crowd,
Raising a roar of response, of love and loathing –
Fat scapegoats stuck with broad rosettes of learning.

I listened and made myself little, still as a mouse
Watching the growling pussies at their antics –
Now I see, in the back row of any classroom,
Sharp impatient eyes, weighing me up for the drop.

Large masks creak. Sir will tear a passion to tatters.
One must pray for unobstructed moments,
For chances to be useful,
Like theirs, old wretches, like theirs.

Fiesta Mask

The raw feast rages in its fierce buffoons,
Flares in hot air. Calliope blares red.
Streamers, confetti, squeakers and fat balloons.
Here comes a great, big, daft, nid-nodding head –

A painted acre of face, a carnival grin,
With snouting nostrils, glistening carbuncles:
And children cringe, afraid to be sucked in
And eaten up by wickedest of uncles.

Once upon a time, some small boys found
In the next daylight's debris, after the revels
Had guttered down – the giant stretched on the ground,
Stupid in drunken sleep. The young devils

Began by throwing pebbles to sound the big head,
To find just what was under the disguise –
Started to claw the cardboard into shreds,
And one little bastard kept kicking at plaster eyes.

They battered at the craters he was breathing beer through,
Tore cheeks away in chunks. He didn't groan.
Soon there were ragged gaps enough to peer through.
And the squealing stopped. As if they'd been turned to stone.

Railway Pieces

1 *Poster for London Transport*

Science-fiction, tattered and out-of-date
Bequeaths a landscape where our bodies move.
Flambeaux, portentous down the escalator,
Parade an avenue in *art nouveau*,
Herald a progress – Way for Captain Nemo!
Constricted corridors and halls of neuter wind –
How many years since they were tarted up –
Washed over in new styles of architecture
On top of Dali-Doré-picturesque?
Trough-of-the-wave-stuff now, in fashion's hell.

'Nor are we out of it,' we mutter, pushed.
Official tormentors swarm, in diligent hats,
Clicking pedantic pincers. MIND THE GAP.
Lose the way and miss the underground connection,
All boredom condensed, fused to a helpless minute
Of pacing a grey slab at OXFORD CIRCUS
Between banked stares of glaring ikons –
Strenuous BEER and nubile CORSETS
AMPLEX GOD OVALTINE ELECTRIC RAZORS –
Only a stop away from TOTTENHAM COURT ROAD.

2 Hypochondriac Reading Newspaper

The sun-lit surface shrugs. An easy day...
No extra effort needed
To keep down monsters coiling underneath,
The hunched muscles writhing
In private hells, the gas-lit punishment cells.

Strained morning-face in the train
Keeps stoic lines, though careful to have ready
Accommodation, tolerant knowing eyes:
Only eager to relax, be safe a little,
Melt to a decent shape in smiles.

But always eyes find words to jerk fear back,
Something gross to be afraid of,
A thought to block the sun:
A twist in the dimensions
That can't be laughed away or worked away.

The ghosts are dwindled, only to re-form
More brassily efficient:
(Pale SYPHILIS deflated, pinked by penicillin –)
And see they all come back, infectious breaths,
Compulsive gripes to hold us gibbering

Bold CANCER, famous BOMB, blonde TELEVISION,
And statistical pressure of PUBLIC OPINION.

3   *The Songs*

Continuous, a medley of old pop numbers –
Our lives are like this. Three whistled bars
Are all it takes to catch us, defenceless
On a District Line platform, sullen to our jobs,
And the thing stays with us all day, still dapper, still Astaire,
Still fancy-free. We're dreaming while we work.

Be careful, keep afloat, the past is lapping your chin.
South of the Border is sad boys in khaki
In 1939. And J'attendrai a transit camp,
Tents in the dirty sand. Don't go back to Sorrento.
Be brisk and face the day and set your feet
On the sunny side always, the sunny side of the street.

After a week of fog, a mild bright winter morning.
Here I am in the train, reading Wordsworth to work
Without any impatience. Eyes stray from those pastures
And through the window find WANDSWORTH a peaceable beast
    enough,
Sprawling and arching a brick back in the sun.
And look again at the others, no longer lifeless
Waxwork heads nodding, fixed stares at newsprint:
Their eyes are mild with interest, wander without anxiety,
Without any impatience. The pressure is off.
There is no strain in the morning under the blue sky.
Have we ever doubted heaven? Why, already here...
At least, until we get to WATERLOO...

A Game of Royal Families
From the French of Jean Pervert

(for Alan Brownjohn)

First of all the King. Where's the King of Hearts?
The King is in his counting-house, of course.
And what is he doing, is he counting
His money up, just as one would expect?
No, he's eating tarts, a great plateful
Of jam-tarts, blood-coloured jam-tarts
Stolen to frame the Knave of Hearts.
(He'll have to look to his muttons, that one.)
Then the Queen, what's she up to? Where but in her parlour?
But not with the Knave of Hearts, oh no!
The Queen's mouth is sticky with honey only
When the Jack of Clubs roughs her up.
No need to ask about His Grace
Of Diamonds and His Grace of Spades –
In the linen closet, as usual,
Enjoying unnatural relations with each other.
But where's the swaggerer, Knave of Hearts, where's he?
Where would you think, he's in the garden
With the maid.
But that's no alibi, that won't save his head.
They'll get at her through her father, the hump-backed joker,
And she'll tell some story about a bird from the sky
Pecking her nose off.
But what this lot don't reckon on –
The people think her baby something special –
When he grows up there'll be a revolution –
Hurrah! Hurrah! Hurrah! Hurrah! Hurrah!

A Prodigal Son for Volpone

Conspicuous consumption? Why, Volpone
Would splash it around as if he could afford it,
Wore himself out for his craft, a genuine phoney,
Who only wanted, gloatingly, to hoard it.

His son had sprung like a mushroom, pale in an alley.
Reluctant, they had to unload the stuff on him.
To cook the accounts, got Mosca back from the galleys –
These lawyers worried that the heir looked dim.

What was he, now, to do with all this gold?
His father had withered in prison because of it.
Root of all evil, he'd always been told
By scholars who'd brought him up. Get shot of the lot of it.

Gloomy vaults, cram-full roof-high with piles
Of metal and stone and paper shoved into sacks:
A great city's sewer, bustling golden miles
Swollen for carnival. Must give it back,

Somehow get rid of it, be a big spender.
The tradesmen knew of a new purse spilling around.
Not a junk-shop in Venice that wasn't stripped of its splendour,
Not a period-piece, not an objet d'art to be found.

How richly the monde assembled at his parties,
How thickly clustered in slow gilded whirls!
Sensitive businessmen and butch aesthetic hearties,
Senile young statesmen, faint expensive girls.

'Spend it faster?' He'd pay on the nail for their answers.
A patron's deep-waving harvest was quick to be seen.
A sculptor in barbed-wire, a corps of Bulgarian dancers,
Three liberal reviews and a poetry magazine.

Mosca's smirk broadened. The Foundation showed a profit.
How white and stammering now our Volponetto!
'G-give it to the city. S-see the poor get some of it.'
He vanished aboard a waiting vaporetto.

For one odd halfpenny, Mosca broke on the rack.
The Senate's liver was hardened with golden wine.
Some money drained to the poor. The young man never came back.
Last heard of, was herding swine, or turned to swine.

To Celebrate Eddie Cantor

The flesh is brittle, alas,
And ever-modish time, that fiend, is slee:
The Goldwyn Girls of Nineteen Thirty-Three
Also must go, must fade beyond nostalgia,
Vanish when celluloid crackles.

That year, not less constrained,
We strained the other way to find the future –
Eager and awkward, tried to look sixteen,
Be full initiates into the life of the time
And shuffle into the LYRIC, the local flea-pit.
We howled and whistled, fidgets on iron seats.

Our coming-in was brisk to music
Strident through raucous light along the slanting floor,
Underfoot rubbish and everywhere sweet disinfectant
Stinking like LADIES and GENTLEMEN –
The whole place blatant and blaring,
Usherettes sullen and louts obstreperous.

And, slumping back in seats, to see a flick,
Shadows to look at shadows, not expecting luck,
Amazed then, caught in your outrageous joy,
Dear Eddie!
                    Blank looming screen
And then you whirled from its imagined wings –
A small impassioned man who could hardly wait for his music,
A master, from Vaudeville, an accomplished master.

Voice soaring in gleeful lubricity,
Scandalous coloratura at full tilt!
Excited wide eyes rolling
And hands that have to clap that joy's too much.
Energy, wanton small bright ball
Leaping on top of the fountain –
Living water, extravagant
Flooding and cleansing the movie-house.

No endless exits down the sad perspectives,
The avenues of infinite regrets,
For you, Sir, No Sircc!
Palmy Days, ample a blue sky
And the gross bull lulled to an euphoric calm,
Contented cows, O Don Sebastian –
The lineaments of gratified desire
Making whoopee with the whooping red-skins.

Thinly we rustled, ears of unripe corn –
You could have gathered us up in the palms of your hands.
Singing and dancing, you came out more than real,
Potent Revivalist, strong drink for shadows –
For you at the end of the picture
Bunches and baskets of flowers, all of them girls.

Ode to Groucho

1 *Invocation*

Pindarick, a great gorblimey Ode
Soaring on buzzard wings, ornate,
Or tottering titanic on feet of clay,
It would have to be, to be adequate –
With the neo-gromboolian overtones
And the neo-classic gimmicks:
Pat gags cadenced from 'Mauberley'
In platinum-plated timing,
And tendrils convolvulating
To clutch the dirty cracks and hold the house up!

O flaking Palladian Palladium!
On a back-cloth rattled by oom-pah –
All our nostalgias, Hey there! the old vaudeville circuit.
Proscenium buttressed with brutal truths
Where sleek myths lean in manneristic attitudes,
Chalk-white in the chastest diction,
Sequined with glittering metaphysicality.
And massive ambiguities
Endlessly rocking a whole way of life.

2 *Presence*

What you had was a voice
To talk double-talk faster,
Twanging hypnotic
In an age of nagging voices –
And bold eyes to dart around
As you shambled supremely,
Muscular moth-eaten panther!

Black eyebrows, black cigar,
Black painted moustache –
A dark code of elegance
In an age of nagging moustaches –
To discomfit the coarse mayor,
Un-poise the suave headmaster,
Reduce all the old boys to muttering fury.

A hero for the young,
Blame if you wish the human situation –
Subversivest of con-men
In an age of ersatz heroes:
Be talkative and shabby and
Witty; bully the bourgeois;
Act the obvious phoney.

3   *Apotheosis*

Slickness imposed on a rough beast,
A slouching beast and hypochondriac.

Great Anarch! Totem of the lot,
All the shining rebels

(Prometheus, of course, and that old pauper
Refusing cake from Marie Antoinette,
And Baudelaire's fanatical toilette,
And Rimbaud, striding off to Africa,
And Auden, scowling at a cigarette...)

Bliss was it etc. Smartish but fair enough.
We stammered out our rudenesses

O splendid and disreputable father!

Headmaster: Modern Style

(for Philip Hobsbaum)

I

This leader's lonely, all right! He sees to that.
Inspectors, governors, parents, boys and staff –
His human instruments – are all shocked back
From the stunned area round him, sound of his voice.
Wag, wag, of tongue is his wig and his weapon
Raking a stamping ground
For his mannikin's hard-headed strut in a neat grey suit,
For those liquorice allsorts, his barrow-boy eyes
(Shrewdness and suspicion go on and off like traffic-lights)
For the maggot-twitch at the end of his almost endless nose.

II

What a nuisance the little man is!
If two stay behind, to paint scenery
And he offers to help
They toss for who does the painting and who listens to him.

III

'Snitch', the boys call him, 'Snitch' or 'Conk'.
'Rats', he calls them, 'Slackers, Dirty Rats'.

IV

No Room for Gothic ghosts here
In the gleam of the public-urinal-type 1870 tiles –
There's a really up-to-date practical talking poltergeist
Resounds all day throughout the shameful building
That can't be prettied up, although they try:
It talks to the contractors' men on their small jobs –
He must slow them up.

V

And what does he talk about? Well, what was it?
Imagine a five act opera with only one voice,
Continuous recitativo secco monologue –
But in real life? And what is it all about?

It is for something and it isn't for you
It isn't something he'd want your opinion for
He's got it all worked out, he knows his line
Anecdote and anecdote and anecdote
To keep him talking, not to listen to you
Slugged into acquiescence by his knowing drone.

VI

He buzzes like pin-table-lights, flashing enormous scores
In disregard of what the ball is doing.
How does he keep it going?

Well, R.A.F. He was in the R.A.F.
A ground-staff commission in the R.A.F.
On heat with reminiscence on Battle of Britain day.
Knew how to get what they wanted, anything, any equipment
They knew their stuff, all right, when they occupied Germany
With nudges, winks, and Cockney chuckles.

And apparently spent all their time in the mess discussing religion.
That put him on to Christ. That's where your ethics comes from.
(He rehearses an operetta with a cane in his hand.)

Knows his way round any committee
Officials and contracts and regulations,
How to get round them, how to get praised for it.

VII

This poem goes on pattering just like he does.
This is the way to elicit expensive equipment.
The burgess are pleased to be stung for expensive equipment
(Quite a lot of the poor little wretches can't read)
New vistas in education, shining technical vistas

Showers and lathes and ropes and coats of paint
A new laboratory, new wood-work shop, new metal-work shop
Shelves in the library, elegant functional tombs
Where WILLIAM, BIGGLES, BUNTER rest in peace.

The boys should be grateful for all the equipment they're getting.

49

VIII
Let's turn aside
As Augustine might turn from a chapter on pride and concupiscence,
And consider poor Joe, Conk's deputy.

Joe does administration. It does for him. He's done by it.
Nothing comes right. He mutters about it.
Prometheus-Conk goes free. Joe gets the vultures.

Chief eunuch of the stock-room! Emperor of pen-nibs –
Footprints that vanish in the snow from Moscow!
And blotting-paper gone – to stuff the dykes?
The chalk they eat, the ink they drink....

O the staff are a sore trial to poor old Joe!
They won't add their registers right. Their dinner-money's hopeless.
They will ask for stock on a Wednesday.
They send their classes down before the bell goes....

Joe's tight face sits filling up the forms
And his small office shakes. A voice next door is sounding
About Christ and committees and polar exploration.

No doubt that Joe has still to be working, working, working.
And the Head to be talking, talking, talking.

IX
On Speech Day
The Chairman of the governors makes a speech.
An athlete makes a speech and gives out prizes.
The headmaster's speech is the longest.

Sea-shanties this year? No,
NON NOBIS DOMINE.

X
Let's finish this business off.
Let's take the backwardest class, 2E say,
Up the last stairs, to the Art Room....

They are so eager to do something
That they stop being awkward, knocking things over, sit still and
attend.

Give out the clay. Never mind if they get it all over their clothes,
All over the desks, all over the floor.

'Right! Now I want you to make a headmaster.'

They will solemnly prod into life long-snitched headmaster-dolls.

Nothing crude like sticking pins?
Well all right, we will stick pins then, but also
Shove in chewed bubble-gum to make his eyes.

Give him a surplice of toffee-paper and hymn-book leaves.
Let bottle-tops stinking of yesterday's milk be gathered for his medals.

Ode to Himself

Go on, good monkey, make your bow, be me.
Appear as the polite one, the sensitive
Shy one, awkward but helpful,
Monkey of wisecracks, monkey who knows the words.

This social creature must ignore
All his disgraces, all the deplorable monkeys;
They antic behind his back as if they were at home:
Evil-tempered monkey with weak rage,
Envious idle incompetent monkey
A spiteful mimic of more handsome apes,
Belching wasteful monkey, timid
Monkey of tiny dishonesties.

Sad monkey, a self-pitying one,
Unlucky monkey, monkey who was framed
By mean streets in the shabby years –
Poor wretch of a monkey
In the freezing winds of time,
Almost a brass monkey.

Miniature snarling super-ego monkey
Squatting on the shoulder of the gross orang-outang

And stinking cynical monkey
Planning small satisfactions
In face of an abstract nothing –
What a nest of nasty negative monkeys!

II
Safer not postulate a central me
To be ambitious about all this
This chattering toyshopful of monkey puppets.
No puppet-master stoops
To curb their messy antics: monkey business
Must be endured
If only as talk in the head.

To watch is possible: therefore you must watch.
Sit down. Sit still. Eat your damned apple up.
The largest virtue is to pay attention,
Then watch intently, watcher in the dark –
Watch how a jangling piano-range of strings
Dangles a reigning Kong for every minute,
Wearing your shirt and tie, your beard, your spectacles,
Inflections of your voice and gestures of your hands,
Grimaces and grimaces and grimaces.

Old monkeys never die, fight back and never die.
They might fade away if you watch them.

And some already folding up their strings
Will lie down neatly in a cardboard box.
R.I.P. monkey. Then again, R.I.P. monkey.

New beasts keep crowding in the wings.
Here come the vulgarest clowns, red-cheeked baboons
With their peanuts and bananas.
Out-stare them. Staunchly watch.

III
The legends say the monkeys drift to sleep
Under clear scrutiny of evening sky,
Puff into cloud-shapes, fade away

And branches prick, impressive silhouette,
Pattern of monkey-puzzle tree.

Reasons for Refusal

Busy old lady, charitable tray
Of social emblems: poppies, people's blood –
I must refuse, make you flush pink
Perplexed by abrupt No-thank-you.
Yearly I keep up this small priggishness,
Would wince worse if I wore one.
Make me feel better, fetch a white feather, do.

Everyone has list of dead in war,
Regrets most of them, e.g.

Uncle Cyril; small boy in lace and velvet
With pushing sisters muscling all around him,
And lofty brothers, whiskers and stiff collars;
The youngest was the one who copped it.
My mother showed him to me,
Neat letters high up on the cenotaph
That wedding-caked it up above the park,
And shadowed birds on Isaac Watts' white shoulders.

And father's friends, like Sandy Vincent;
Brushed sandy hair, moustache, and staring eyes.
Kitchener claimed him, but the Southern Railway
Held back my father, made him guilty.
I hated the khaki photograph,
It left a patch on the wallpaper after I took it down.

Others I knew stick in the mind,
And Tony Lister often –
Eyes like holes in foolscap, suffered from piles,
Day after day went sick with constipation
Until they told him he could drive a truck –
Blown up with Second Troop in Greece:
We sang all night once when we were on guard.

And Ken Gee, our lance-corporal, Christian Scientist –
Everyone liked him, knew that he was good –
Had leg and arm blown off, then died.
Not all were good. Gross Corporal Rowlandson

Fell in the canal, the corrupt Sweet-water,
And rolled there like a log, drunk and drowned.
And I've always been glad of the death of Dick Benjamin,
A foxy urgent dainty ballroom dancer –
Found a new role in military necessity
As R.S.M. He waltzed out on parade
To make himself hated. Really hated, not an act.
He was a proper little porcelain sergeant-major –
The earliest bomb made smithereens:
Coincidence only, several have assured me.

In the school hall was pretty glass
Where prissy light shone through St George –
The highest holiest manhood, he!
And underneath were slain Old Boys
In tasteful lettering on whited slab –
And, each November, Ferdy the Headmaster
Reared himself squat and rolled his eyeballs upward,
Rolled the whole roll-call off an oily tongue,
Remorselessly from A to Z.

Of all the squirmers, Roger Frampton's lips
Most elegantly curled, showed most disgust.
He was a pattern of accomplishments,
And joined the Party first, and left it first,
At OCTU won a prize belt, most improbable,
Was desert-killed in '40, much too soon.

His name should burn right through that monument.

No poppy, thank you.

Dreams of Evasion

I

Deeper and deeper into softer moss
Like rolling downs, but swamp, electric-green
Velvetest counterpane but deeper in

Reeds pricking, sinuous knitting-needles, bunched
Further and deeper in to buzzing confusion
Where flowers eat burnished insects

Tufted sods sink, bristle, go soft
Stamp if you like, tread something flat
Shod feet will cut sharp shapes, but now

Footprints are filling vaguely with
Seeping, spread to shapes of bruises
Sucking is always starting under your feet

II

Water haze dazzles, spits on face
Flickering adders, threads of streams
Stitch, stitch, a brilliance, nets of spiteful talk
Incessant glitter and chatter, theft of soil

Zips gripping, streams bite, bite their way
Urgent to the river. There it lolls
A glint, through greasy banks. And nudges
It has eaten its contours into smiling curves

III

Must get away, must not get wet or dirty
Always a way out, always a bridge
Round the next bend, before the silver sewage
Dimples to whirlpools, piles to a weir
Be clever, find the fussy steps to reach a
Safe structure strutting, riveted in air

A saving thought commits, betrays
To muscles bulging twisted, sickening strides
Struggle for balance on the shining slopes
Of banks of slime
Straining to hold a distance from yourself
Blur lurching up, self in a mirror of mud

IV
On to the multipurpose bridge
Ambitious architecture vast hotel
Delicate metal blue-print convolution
Closet catwalk ingle oubliette
Ballrooms glaring jading chandeliers
(Somebody's got to swing)
Bookwalled dens lined charts of Yarmouth say
And footman, footman, footman phoning columns
Frequent in alcoves
Tip the Vice-Chancellor something handsome
And pump the Padre's palm before you're topped
Climb, crawl, clamber, stroll or stride tiptoe
Polished corridors to priestholes
Stammer up mile-wide winding marble stairs
To bedroom, bedroom, bedroom, royal bedroom
(A good chap in a suit will arrange everything)
Avoid gymnastic apparatus, sides of ships
And small back rooms with private guillotines
Up and down in the lift from unmade bed to unmade bed
Through honeycombed conveniences slithered with shit

The ladder with the mathematic steps
(Ten seconds to solve each equation)
Leads to the gilt chairs of the Senate Chamber
Through a mouse-slit in the ceiling

One's scared to fall and does of course and
Screams right through the drop
                                    Falls
And hopes to wake up

Winter Coming On
A caricature from Laforgue

(for Peter Porter)

Fine feelings under blockade! Cargoes just in from Kamchatka!
Rain falling and falling and night falling
And how the wind howls...
Hallowe'en, Christmas, New Year's Day
Sodden in drizzle – all my tall chimneys –
Industrial smoke through the rain!

No sitting down, all the park-benches are wet.
It's finished, I tell you, till next season.
Park-benches wet and all the leaves rust-eaten,
Horns and their echoes – dying, dying...

Rally of rain-clouds! Procession from the Channel –
You certainly spoiled our last free Sunday.

Drizzles:
And in wet woods the spiders' webs
Weigh down with rain-drops: and that's their lot.
O golden delegates from harvest festivals,
Broad suns from cattle-shows,
Where have they buried you?
This evening a sun lies, shagged, on top of the hill,
On a tramp's mattress, rags in the gorse –
A sun as white as a blob of spittle
On tap-room saw-dust, on a litter of yellow gorse,
Of yellow October gorse.
And the horns echo and call to him –
Come back! Won't you come back?

View halloo, Tally-ho...Gone away.
O oratorio chorus, when will you be done?
Carrying on like mad things...
And there he lies, like a torn-out gland on a neck,
Shivering, with no one by.
Tally-ho, then, and get on with it.
It's good old Winter coming, we know that.

By-passes empty, turnings on main roads
With no Red Riding Hood to be picked up.
Ruts from the wheels of last month's traffic –
Quixotic tram-lines to the rescue of
Cloud-patrols scurrying
Bullied by winds to transatlantic sheep-folds.
Get a move on, it's the well-known season coming, now.
And the wind last night, on top of its form,
Smashing suburban front-gardens – what a mess!
Disturbing my night's sleep with dreams of axes.

These branches, yesterday, had all their dead leaves –
Nothing but compost now, just lying about.
Dear leaves of various shapes and sizes
May a good breeze whirlpool you away
To lie on ponds, decorative,
To glow in the park-keeper's fire,
To stuff ambulance mattresses, comforts
For our soldiers overseas.

Time of year, time of year: the rust is eating,
The rust is gnawing long miles of ennui,
Telegraph-wires along main roads, deserted.

Horns, again horns…the echoes dying,
Dying…
Now changing key, going north
With the North Wind, Wagnerian,
Up to all those bloody skalds and Vikings…

Myself, I can't change key; too many echoes!
What beastly weather! Goodbye autumn, goodbye ripeness…
And here comes the rain with the diligence of an angel.
Goodbye harvest, good-bye baskets for nutting,
And Watteau picnics under the chestnut trees.
It's barrack-room coughing again,
The landlady's horrible herbal tea –
It's TB in the garden suburb,
All the sheer misery of satellite towns.

Wellingtons, long underwear, cash chemists, dreams,
Undrawn curtains over verandas, shores
Of the red-brick sea of roofs and chimney-pots,
Lamp-shades, tea and biscuits, all the picture papers –
You'll have to be my only loves!
(And known them, have you? ritual more portentous
Than the sad pianos tinkling through the dusk,
The registrar's returns of births and deaths,
In small type weekly in the press.)

No! It's the time of year, and this clown of a planet!
O please let the wind, let the high wind
Unknit the bed-socks Time is knitting herself!
Time of year, things tearing, time of year!
O let me every year, every year, just at this time
Join in the chorus, sound the right sour note.

The Ballad Singer at the Pardon of St Anne

(from Corbière)

I

Blessed the barren dunes,
Stark nude like the sea –
And the chapel of Anne-of-Palud
Is crude, too, and holy,

Of St Anne, the Good Gossip,
A granny for young Jesus
In rotting oak beneath a rich
Cope...richer than Croesus.

Beside her, the Virgin is small –
Fragile distaff, waiting for Angelus –
And St Joseph, upstaged, in his niche
Shoves his candle at us.

It's Her Pardon – fun and games and
Mystery – the stubble's hopping with fleas –
Anne, Sainted Ointment, cure-all
For mothers-in-law, and husband's ease.

From the parishes round about,
From Plougastel and Loc-Trudy,
They've arrived already, camping out
Three nights, three days, up till Monday.

Three days, three nights, the salt-marsh blares
With music – the rite's traditional –
Heavenly choir and singing drunks –
Beginneth the SACRED CANTICLE.

II

O Mother, carved out with a chopper
From oak heart, hard and good,
Your gold robe hides a solid Breton
Soul, all one piece, honest wood.

Green crone with a used-up face,
Boulder under the flood,
Fretted by tears of love,
Parched by tears of blood.

You, whose shrivelled breasts
Were plumped again, to carry
A purposeful virginity –
The Virgin Mary.

Proud housekeeper, mistress and servant,
Related to the Almighty,
The poor are pleased to talk to you
For you answer them politely.

A wand for the blind, and crutches
For cripples, arms for the new-born,
A mother for Madame your Daughter –
You've adopted all the forlorn.

Blossom of new maidenhead!
Fruit of wife's swollen udder!
Garden of rest for the widow!
District Nurse for the widower!

Joachim's Arch! O Ancestress!
Four-leaf clover! Mistletoe bough!
Medallion with a rubbed-out face!
Horeb! Jesse's Rod! Our way!

You kept the fire in
And went on with your knitting
As darkness came down round your lap
Where the Child was sitting.

You were there, the one who could cope,
Making garments in Bethlehem,
Still there, stitching the shroud,
Grief-stunned in Jerusalem.

Your face is a wrinkled map
Of crosses – your hair white as linen –
Keep from pedantic evil eyes
The cots of our grandchildren.

The born, the not-yet born,
Bring on, and keep them well,
And smuggle water from your tears
When God isn't looking, to Hell.

Take back little children
In white nightgowns, fading away,
And summon the old who are bored
To the everlasting Sunday.

O growl! The Virgin's Dragon!
Keep the crib safe and secure,
And keep bitching at Joseph
To sweep round the front door.

Pity the girl in the family way
And the small boy lost on the road –
If anyone throws a stone
Change it into bread.

Beacon on sea and on land,
Harbour, stars over heath,
Good Lady, through tempest, through war,
You beckon towards a good death.

Humble; no star at your feet –
Humble and strong to save –
Your veil in the clouds means peril,
Pale halo over the wave.

Those whose lives are a mess
– Begging pardon – sunk in the booze –
Show them the steeple and clock,
The road back to the house.

Fire the Christians hereabouts
With your own zeal, gentle and chaste,
And gather your simples, Wise Woman,
To soothe the horned beast.

Be an example to housewives
Of work and fecundity –
And say hullo to our relations
Already in eternity.

We'll line up an army of candles –
Spermaceti – the best – all the way
Round your chapel. We'll celebrate
Low mass at the break of day.

Keep our hearths safe
From spells and folk who are spiteful...
We'll give you at Easter
Flax, a whole distaff-full.

If our bodies stink on earth
Your grace is a bath for our good:
Shower on us in this graveyard
Your wholesome odour of sainthood.

Till next year, then. Here's your candle,
(Three half-crowns it's cost me).
Respects to Madame the Virgin,
Not forgetting the Holy Trinity.

III
And the faithful, in penitent nightshirts,
– St Anne, have pity, please –
Drag themselves round the church
Three times, on their knees.

And go on to drink the waters,
Miraculous now, from the hole
Where scabby Jobs have bathed...
Your faith has made you whole.

Down there they hold their suppers,
The wretched, Jesus's brethren,
And you won't see any miracles,
But real holes: Put your finger in...

On their hurdles they look like saints,
With scarlet nimbuses, each one
An owner of extensive sores
Like rubies glinting in the sun.

A barking man with rickets
Just can't stop his arm-stump's twitch –
Can't help elbowing the epileptic
Having a fit in the same ditch.

By a tree-trunk, mistletoe-bitten,
Stands a man with an ulcer that bites –
And a mother and daughter are dancing –
Choreography by St Vitus.

A father heats up a poultice
For a small son who's not thriving:
A boy owes a lot to his father –
The chancre earns their living.

There's an idiot since he was born,
An angel-blasted simpleton,
Ecstatic in his innocence –
The simple are close to heaven.

Watch, passer-by, all passes...but
The idiot's stare is stone and firm –
He must be in a state of grace,
For grace is outside time.

Among the crowd after evensong,
When the holy water's sprayed us,
A corpse sticks out, alive, a long
Leper...relic of the crusaders.

Then those who the kings of France
Used to cure with a touch –
Since France has cut off her kings,
Their God's cut his mercy by that much.

Put something into their bowls –
All our forefathers carried it,
The Fleur-de-Lys of King's Evil
Which these are chosen to inherit.

Miserere then for the junketings
Of these dirty old outcast Bretons...
But stumps can be managed like pincers
And crutches are weapons.

Venture among them, able-bodied,
But take care to keep your fleece on –
Beware of fingers that hook, of legs
Fixed in Kyrie Eleison.

And if you'd be sight-seeing, dear,
Take a look and turn back quick –
From under these scraps of rags
A scrap of flesh might prick.

They're hunting on their own estates
With Arms emblazoned on their skins!
Their hands have the droit de seigneur
Over anything clutched therein.

Offerings heaped – of rotting meat –
Heaven's elect – with death-house features –
They make themselves at home with God
For surely they're his creatures.

They're swarming in the churchyard –
As if the dead mistook the Day
Of Judgement, crawling out from stones
That crush the limbs they drag away.

We've no right to talk – they're sacred.
It's Adam's sin they're punished for.
The Almighty's finger has marked them,
The Almighty's right be praised therefore!

The scapegoats of the bellowing flock,
Loaded with every sin we're at,
God works his anger off on them!
The vicar of St Anne's is fat.

IV

But a palpitating note,
A gasping echo in the breeze,
Cuts across the grumbling drone
Of this walking purgatory.

Keening like a beast in pain,
She stands beside the Calvary,
Half a blind beggar, as it were,
No dog and only one eye. –

A weather-bitten ballad-singer,
Drop a halfpenny in her hat
And she'll do you Abaylar, Wandering Jew,
Or any other old favourite.

O but her song is long-drawn-out,
Complaining like a thing ill-used,
Like a long day with nothing to eat,
So lamentable her blues.

She sings just as she breathes, a bird
Without a nest, with no fine feathers,
Battering blindly as she flies
Round granite God, in granite weather.

She can talk, too, if that matters,
As far as she can see she thinks –
The main road keeps stretching before her –
If she gets hold of sixpence, she drinks.

A woman, oh dear yes – her skirt
Is strings held together by string:
Black teeth grip an empty pipe –
Life is full of excellent things!

Her name? Call her Misery.
Got herself born, somehow, somewhere –
Somewhere, someday will be found dead –
There'll be no fuss, no one will care.

If you come across her, poet,
Humping her army kit-bag –
Please recognise our sister,
Give her a few fills of shag.

You'll see on her furrowed face
A smile crack right across
Like splitting wood, her scaly hand
Make a genuine sign of the cross.

Blind Man's Cries

(from Corbière)

The eye is killed, not numb
A sharpened edge still splits
I'm nailed, but not in the tomb
My eye's got a nail in it
A cruel wedge still splits
An eye that's dead not numb

Deus Misericors
Have mercy on us
A hammer hits my head bang bang
It nailed the cross where Christ did hang
And have mercy upon us
Deus Misericors

Birds that tatter the dead
Stay away from my head
Dear God, you've forsaken me
Golgotha's still breaking me
Wait your time, black doves,
You'll get victual enough

Like a gun-port's hole my wounds
Burn red the whole way round
Like an old woman's gummy grin
Before she puts her false teeth in
Burning, all the way round
Like a gun-port's hole my wounds

Its circles of gold I see
A white sun eating me
Two holes pierced by a spit
Hell fire white-heated it
Rings and rings of gold I see
Fire from heaven devouring me

My marrow twists about
And a tear comes out
All paradise globed there I see
Out of my depths I cry to Thee
My brain-pan seethes about
A sulphur tear comes out

Happy the watch they keep
The good dead fast asleep
Blessed the martyrs chosen
With Jesus and the Virgin
Blissful the watch they keep
Judged, saved, and asleep

Stretched out under the skies
A tall knight lies
In the graveyard's holy ground
His granite sleep is sound
Lucky the stone man lies
With two untroubled eyes

You Breton heaths you stretch
Sallow around me yet
My fingers feel the rosary
And the bone Christ on the tree
Still like a beast I cry
To the dead Breton sky

Democracy
(from Rimbaud)

The colours on parade, dipping past the filthy bricks of this garrison town. Boots, newly issued, stutter on the cobbles; but we can keep step.

We'll be posted overseas, to the big Base Depots. White buildings in long straight lines, like the Big City itself, but with everything laid on, just for us. It'll be the biggest, best-run brothel in the world. If the students riot, it'll be us reservists who're called out.

East of Suez or thereabouts – where the cold beer is grateful to the clay that gurgles it up, and the temper rises nicely after meals. We'll make the black bastards work: leader-writers will talk about the Commonwealth.

Anywhere, to get away from home. Glad to be back in the army, we'll use our loaves, all right. We can't pass exams, but we get our feet under the table. Everyone else can get fucked. Progress we call it.

By – The – Right – Quick – MARCH

Instruction for my Godson
(for William Redgrove)

God help me, I'm supposed to see you're told
All about God the Father. So my beard mutters:
There are always two fathers, one Good and one Bad.
You can't miss the Bad One, he's always around,
Particularly first thing in the morning,
Scruffy and screaming for a razor-blade,
Wondering who to eat up for his breakfast –
He won't eat you however much he shouts.
I'm not trying to sell you bad old Nobodaddy –
Learn to shrug off his sessions on his throne
Farting thunderbolts and belching clouds.

The Good One has a different way with clouds; he watches.
He knows fifty-seven ways at least of looking at them,
He addresses them politely, and his looking
Can hold them still in the sky.

Letter to a Friend

Dear Russ, you're dead and dust. I didn't know.
I've heard it only at removes. For X
Who we detested, passed it on from Y,
For whom we had a jeering kind of fondness –
He read about it in the Old School Journal –
One way of keeping up.

'Organic disease' were the words. Which one?
Which painful monster had you when you died?
As good a life as me, I would have said –
You're one-up now, you smug old bastard:
'Christ, boy,' you say, 'I'm dead now.'
Stop dribbling bubbles of laughter round your pipe.

How many years since both of us owed letters?
Let's offer the usual excuses –
Marriage, of course, wives don't get on,
The housing-shortage, railway fares, etc.,
Weak putting-off, sheer bloody laziness.
We didn't want to say the way things went
Pissed on the hopes we entertained,
Naive, of course, but vivid and still pissed on –
The old gang born again in young careerists –
(Christ, boy, they're reading *The Times* now!)
As if we hadn't known all this before!

Gratitude, now, is what's appropriate.
How glad I am I've had your company!
After an adolescent's silly days
Of idle mornings, hypochondriac afternoons,
Thick skies that frowned and trees that swayed foreboding,
What evenings of relief have set me free!

Evenings of beer and talk, bezique, Tchaikovsky,
Hysterical evenings screeching at dull flicks,
And evenings when we gossiped into movement
The huge grotesques we knew, to keep us sane –
Hadji, Wokko, Nodger hardly knew themselves
And should we meet would start us off again.

'Christ, boy,' you say, 'Listen to this.'
Something new, I expect, about Taverner's sponges,
Drying, between the lying maps, in rows.
The sods today are duller and more utter,
But deadlier, deadlier still.

A formal ending I can't manage.
We've been solemn enough before, at Party meetings,
Constructive, eager, serious, ineffective...
'Yours fraternally,' then. And grin your inverted commas.
Help me to tell the truth and not feel dull.

High Street, Southampton

Mean enough now, re-built, street I once knew,
And tame and bright and tight and wide enough
Now, neat toy-town blocks of boxes, Noddy shops
With plastics wrapped in cellophane for sale.
A shiny hum of traffic with no pulse
Along the concrete now. Time to un-pin
Bravado, unfreeze tears, feel pain.

We missed the climax of excitement
In the old High Street, when it burned:
Twenty-two years led up to this, a loss.
Nineteen Eighteen, Armistice Day
Waves of excitement thundered round my pram,
The crowded skyline bristled in relief,
Shops packed in narrow cliffs rang joy.

But found no Ali Baba word to open
The caves to small boys' lust, each heaven cut off –
(A crimson wedge of steak, coffee to rape a nose,
Vast scented lilies, lobsters, brandy-balls,
Spectrum of ties from which to choose a week –)
The angel plate-glass scolded lack of means,
Banished a school-boy home – tea, homework, bed.

So Speech Day willed a jeering oil to blister
Forty distinguished Old Boys: the Mayor to be strung up.
Militant ARMS FOR SPAIN boards down the High Street,
And DAILY WORKER outside cinemas.
(A fat old bald man sighed, 'Ah! Propaganda!'
And livid neon smirked back from his brow.
And all the Fifty-Shilling Tailors' dummies sneered).

And after Munich put us into heat,
We went on talking, walking up and down,
A Saturday addiction, dear Unreal City!
And *enfin* Betjeman's slim volume came
To prove to us we loved, about to lose;
In small beer, posthumous, glowed wonted fires,
Rake's progress to armed forces of the crown.

Not there, then, in the blast, when flames were eating.
(My parents started walking out of town.)
Came back on leave, amazed, it was all gone,
Nothing was where it was and all was wrong,
And everywhere looked through to green of park,
Vistas to statues or to distant spires.
And scuttled, numb, to pubs still left.

Bar Gate survived, as usual, with its air
Of being left over from some other pageant,
Waiting to be relieved by Ham the Fifth.
Après la guerre, the G.I. saw a slum,
And wished himself in Naples or Berlin.
We met again and told old stories, hastily
Beat it for London, looked for jobs.

It's rough that there's no moral comes from this,
Only excuse for lack of roots.
Where is the Phoenix? Surely there was burning.
With more bravado still, some extra tears,
We just accentuate a usual gap.
Old stories for old friends, then shy away
And pick up, elsewhere, what we can.

Three Days

A pleasant way to finish the war off
At the convalescent Depot at Salerno,
Scrounging, on the Education Staff –
Run Quiz, Tombola, Brains' Trust in the NAAFI,
Give left-wing lectures on the post-war world.
Plenty of cheap, good, spirits in the Sergeants' Mess,
And sea and time enough to swim off hangovers.

Armistice, Italy, was a fine, fine day.
We were awed and excited, suddenly free.
Finito Tedesci. Finito Boum Boum. And no fear now
To be sent up through squalid transit-camps
To front-line mountains, snow and mud and bang.
Sang the RED FLAG again, several times this time –
Alex had brought it off before Montgomery –
And a muscular Glaswegian R.S.M.
Thumped on the bar and glinted through black brows:
'It's victorry for the lads. I'm glad. I'm glad
It's victorry for the worrkers back at home.'
We left the mess and went swimming, drunk in the moonlight.

V.E. Day was a different matter, stale.
Started drinking in the morning, went on all day,
We'd expected this so long, and O.K. this was it,
We were rancid with expectation.
And Churchill wireless-spoke, fatigued. What was it?
Submarine bases, Ireland? What about demobilisation?
And a red-cap sergeant, who nobody trusted,
Lay groaning under a table: 'Four bleeding years!
Churchill! Four bastard years and a half!.
Churchill! etc., etc., etc.,'
True but tedious, we thought.

Next day got up with brass-sick mouth.
We went about our duties, sullenly.

V.J. Day I spent in Halifax, Yorks.,
Wilfrid Pickles' home-town, R.E. Depot.
They had the gall to get us on parade

For a major to tell us the war was over.
It wasn't we weren't pleased the new invention
Had finally finished things off. And no fear now etc.
But there wasn't much celebration, there wasn't much beer in the
     town,
And the locals wouldn't have a lot to do with us.
They'd had time to get used to soldiers, all through the war.

Bell's Elegy

The Bomb's been dropped again, in style, and how!
Fat clouds are worried over the debris.
A patch of blue sky stares. What happens now?
Angels weeping, of course. Mainly for me.

Ode to Psychoanalysis

I

I said to Doctor Hackenbush
During abortive analysis,
'I hate the word, Love.'
I meant parents' unhelpful concern,
I meant they had to bring me up
To work hard and do without money
Just as they had:
I had to be neat and industrious
And flatter any bosses around
With my modest ability to cope.

II

My penis was dangerous, dangerous, dangerous,
Messy and dangerous,
In danger of being cut off.

(My God, the ducks were quacking for it,
And cocks ran round and round without their heads,
My grandmother's cat chased a rabbit's tail on a string.)

My bladder was sadder and madder and badder
When I used to wet the bed.
I remember a cold rubber sheet underneath.
(Dear waters, please, bring back the Flood).

My bowels were a sheer embarrassment,
Holding back in white-faced spite,
And then erupting generosity,
A richness on a social afternoon...

III

I didn't get very far, acting it out
With Doctor Hackenbush.
I developed, he said,
'A massive negative transference,'
So the analysis was cut off
After I hadn't paid him
For over two months –
He took two-fifths of my wages.
(His name wasn't Hackenbush anyway).
I still wanted to kill Stalin
After that. But I felt I'd let Freud down.
The cook would not run the State,
And the State wouldn't wither away,
And psychoanalysis
Was very expensive indeed:
Postpone, for the time being,
The New Jerusalem.

IV

So here I am, in the middle of several paths,
More or less where I've always been
Having survived war and intensive masturbation
Getting away with murder, maybe
But suffering Hell because I'm always overdrawn
At the bank whose manager hovers
Clacking revengeful shears.

Hey there! Nobodaddy!
That's *my* flaming sword...

Manicure

Each fingernail, ugly again,
Must be clipped to a crisp moon.
Ten horny wedges,
A city's dirt under the edges,
Could sharpen to ten weapons,
Razors, flick-knives – mustn't happen.
An urbane law,
Not red in tooth and claw,
Says what nails are for:
Combing the eyebrows neatly,
Scratching the skin discreetly,
Squeezing blackheads, scraping corns from toes,
And picking one's nose.

Techniques for Détente

Que messieurs les assassins commencent...

1

Would have been pleased to help
Harvest the lamp-posts –

Each lean aristo's arrogant nose
Slowly describe circles,
And hard-boiled glares take in
New cycles, brash phenomena –

Each committeeing bourgeois
Feel rope through folds of fat
Neck – pressing up a grin
Around accountant mouth –

Once. But it's changed. Changed utterly.
We must love one another or die. A terrible
Beauty is born.
                  Jesus Christ, mates, I know
It's terrible. We'll have to put up with it.

2

Summing up and sending off to swing
Hardens facial muscle and
Sends nerves twittering,
Makes bowels plunge. Pass
The port. Tell me, My Lord, about it.

I share your nightmares, Sir –
Mr Home Secretary.

I've got one, thanks, Mr Pierrpoint.
But you have one with me
But let's agree it's disgusting.

3

I dreamed a heap of corpses.
They were vile and wicked.
I am an assassin.
I begin.

4

Thank God for the House of Lords
And the embassy to Outer Mongolia.

Let Bomber Harris
Enjoy his front garden.
Give him first prize for lupins.

Let all the old men cultivate their gardens.
It's about time.

Let them wander up and down trim paths
Fantastically wreathed in sweet peas.

5

I nominate Mao
For the MCC.
He'll hit em for six.

I've taken up Mah Jong.

6

But the terrifying thing
Is houses,
A stake in the country.

One good down payment
And wages of a steady job –
A bloody-minded feudal lord is in,
In number fifty three.

Something to hand down.
Television performers
Become household serfs.
(I've seen suburban streets in Durban,
Nice people liking things nice.)

Dismal boxes voting tory.

A grip on the earth's crust –
Risky bravado.

7
Fellow citizens,
Forgive yourselves
Please. Forgive yourselves, please,
Thoroughly. Forgive your lack of status.
You'll never be impressive like new office blocks.

I break off here
To forgive myself a long and dismal list.

8
I forgive Stephen Spender.
I forgive Philip Toynbee.
I even forgive
Christopher Logue.

I award each simultaneously a Nobel Prize.

9
Why, Mr Vxxxxxxx.,
How well you look.

Your holiday
Has done you good.

You must be full of beans.
The girls won't leave you alone.

(They'll shag him to death,
Them high yaller gals.)

    10
How about it, Comrade K.?
What about Comrade Bukharin?

...And the big one you don't test?
Call it Lef Davidovitch.

    11
I will sit down beside
The Earl Russell
To talk about D.H. Lawrence.

Poor sod, he's dead. Done down.

    12
'Acts of injustice done
Between the setting and the rising sun
In history lie like bones, each one.'

Thus Auden, on F.6.

Well. Yes. Perhaps. However...

Zen for William Empson

God nowadays spreads thinner than you think,
Is pretty relaxed, permits anything.
Stay quiet and at last you want to sing.
There's black and white and who knows which will stink?

We're all nut-cases now, and who kills whom?
Eichmann killed all the Jews by accident,
Killing goes with each historic event,
Hiroshima's bomb brought all the troops home.

We continue to work and eat, and keep
Begetting each other. Call it Society,
Years of doing things wrong. However

We all know we're near heaven when we sleep.
And learn discrimination by satiety?
Sign for *satori* on the never-never.

Grass, alas

Corn, actually, alas
                         stuck in their crops
Had to clean the grains out
                              with feeling fingers
After I'd lopped the heads
                             of these two pigeons
With kitchen scissors.
Had kept them hanging
                        three days as instructed
Over the kitchen sink.
                          I'd put paper bags round
To conceal
               the pretty pigeons hanging
From my two daughters
                    when they did the washing up.
Then I plucked them
               plucked the small close feathers
From the plump fed breast.
                    I cut the wings off because
There was no point plucking
                 where there was no meat.
And then I drew them, that is
                 pulled their guts out
Through the arse-hole
             (having got drunk before
This loss of virginity)
               and managed not to
burst the gall-bladder.

In the cooking
               I spread myself:
                Salt, black pepper, garlic
                Celery powder, bay leaves
                Mixed herbs and tarragon
                Two spoonfuls of red wine
                An Oxo cube and water
                Regulo 2, three hours
And sealed the corpses by frying
                       before I put them in the casserole.

They were all right.
                    We ate them with
Enjoyment.
             Quite a lot of solid meat
On those small bones
                  but there was too much gravy
Too strongly flavoured
                 no good to keep it.
Cookery, cookery,
            quanto mi costi.

With Heads Uncovered

I'm glad I heard him speak
In a school-hall in Brentford

A few months before he died.
When he arrived the meeting came alive,

The candidate cut short his sensible words,
The party stalwarts cheered and stood and clapped and cheered.

He made a very good speech
Though only school-hall sized.

He twinkled and made little jokes.
He was plump and pink like Santa Claus.

He kept stopping for small coughs
And gaily complained of not being well

And his voice had a cutting edge
When he spoke of the DAILY EXPRESS.

(Among the journalists present one noticed
Mr Muggeridge, a skull, grinning.)

But this was the miner's son,
One of London's best-dressed men,

Who employed George Orwell
To run TRIBUNE's arts-end.

One is reluctant to trust a politician.
Nye Bevan more than most perhaps.
He'll not be easily replaced alas.

David Guest

Well O.K., he was wrong
Getting killed in Spain
Like that. Wal Hannington
Sat and tried to argue him out of going.
He was wrong, he was wrong,
The angel has not descended, the state
Hasn't the faintest chance of withering away,
And nobody is sure which way Hegel is up any more.
He was the greatest hero I've met because he was brave,
And would argue with anybody,
And could interest people because he was interested –
If he was so bloody interested he should have gone on talking, gone
    on talking,
Something might have been talked out.
Near to a saint, he should not have got himself killed,
Thereby making himself an ineffectual angel, a moth.
The Professor of economics was right:
He just couldn't keep still at a public meeting,
He would keep turning round and standing up to see what was
    happening and who was talking,
And this was probably how the bullet got him in the trenches at
    Jarama.

Gabriel Péri
(from Paul Éluard)

A man is killed, he had no defences
But his arms welcoming life
A man is killed, he saw no other road
But one where rifles are detested
A man is killed and goes on fighting
Against death, giving up, forgetting

Everything he wanted
We wanted too
Still want it today
Simple happiness sun shining
Down on hearts and eyes
Simple justice on earth

There are words to go on living for
Innocent words like warmth loyalty
Love and justice. The word freedom
The word child the word gentleness
Flower names and fruit names
The word courage the word inventiveness
The words brother and comrade
And place names where we've been
Names of women names of friends
Let's add the name of Péri
Péri has died for what keeps us alive
Comrade, we'll say, his breast is full of holes
But thanks to him we know each other better
Comrades, we'll say to ourselves, his living hope

Gabriel Péri was foreign editor of L'Humanité, *and was shot as a hostage by the Nazis in 1941.* [M.B.]

Verdi at Eighty

1

My brides are ravished away, are ravished away,
Two Leonoras, Gilda, Violetta,
One swaggering tenor has taken them,
One death seduced them to fever.

I have contrived a basso politics
To hunt him down, conspired
Through trio and quartette, strong situations,
Needled him on to my avenging sword.

2

How shall a wicked, fat, old man be saved?
Connive with the women, incessant giggles and whispers.
He must be re-baptised in muddy water
And wash the district's dirty linen with him.
The wine will chirrup, an insect in old veins.
Ready then assume the sacrificial horns,
Grovel in terror before the Fairy Queen,
So that, our hope, lost lovers may re-join:
Nanetta find a tenor in the woods.
The festival will glow in basso nimbus of laughter.

Requiem for Norman Cameron

Becoming, for your death-bed, an R.C.,
Disposing neatly of N1, 2, 3,
One each to Heaven, Hell and Purgatory –
A thorough-going eccentricity
Imposed a pattern, stilled the flames
Raging outside and in and in between.

Still, lucky for us, your voice haunts
Under the hag, beneath the visiting moon.

Midsummer

It gets a bit wild
After three hot days
Even in England.
One is glad to see
Convolvulus
Get in there among
Pink civic roses...

Leonora

Small female cat, your tortoise-shell coat
Gently goes up and down now you're asleep.
The trouble you've cost us while you've been on heat,
Demanding to be let out at all hours,
Missing your morning liver,
To join the ruined choir of Toms outside.
Now you're asleep, relaxed and grubby,
Neat and detached.

I'll find your ping-pong ball before you wake,
Start advertising kittens for good homes.

Miss Moore on Madison Avenue

White cats recline
on carpets, rich,
purring like Ispahan.
Carpets are manufactured
to advertise cats.

Get your cat to-
day. It doesn't
have to be white. It would
look well on any old rug.
A tabby is fine.

D

In Memoriam: J.B. Leishman

1

He was no good as a lecturer,
Droned through his notes.
As an appearance he counted, though –
Great beak of a Dante nose,
Coarse black Pre-Raphaelite beehive of hair,
Matthew Arnold side-whiskers,
And lumbering body mounted often
In ginger-checkered tweed plus-fours
On a district-nurse type bicycle.

It demanded a vast umbrella, black.

2

(His Rilke
Must have influenced
Auden's sonnets.

His was the first fame
I ever brushed against –
And nicest possibly.)

3

He held his Wednesday evenings
With a gramophone whose loudspeaker
Was broad and craggy as himself.
He would play whatever people asked for
(Somebody naive would ask for
The overture to *Barber of Seville*
Or else the après-midi of a faun –
And then some prig would bring in Bach.)

It was there I first heard
Figaro, Così fan tutte, Zauberflöte
Falstaff, Otello. And songs by Duparc.
He took care to provide libretti for everybody,
But for some reason didn't care for *Don Giovanni*.

An early Glyndebourne attender –
I can only just imagine that clumsy body
Crammed into a dress-suit.

4
I asked him once
With undergraduate pertness
What had Coleridge achieved.

He replied by reciting
'Ode to Dejection'
In a basso voice that trembled.

5
He died by
Walking off an Alp.

6
Once his pipe was burning his tongue.
He made himself a hookah (narguilé, hubble-bubble)
From the two ends of it
And a chemistry flask and rubber tubing.

7
Three things I still copy –
His courteous use of 'Surely' –
'Well', to start an opinion asked for –
And maniac cackle of laughter, crescendo.

From The Irregular Stanzas of Don Senilio
(for Peter Redgrove)

I

'It seems to me now a long time since
I was excited about anything.
I fill my insides with old man's bitter
And feel sour besides. How frail I feel.
And if I stammer now it's not young heat
Baffled, but an inefficient cricket
That never learned the use of its thin limbs
To make proper sounds. Fric, fric, hélas, fric, fric.'
Thus Don Senilio scribbled a climacteric.

II

A leisure morning sits him at his window
To watch grotesques outside. And he collects
An old man puffing, Sellars in a bit part,
An orange matron's parody of slacks.
Those children are too loud. And a great
Biscuit box of a lorry parks outside
And he can't see, puts gramophone records on.
A very old man might sit like this,
Remembering Dan Leno, Marie Lloyd.

III

Does he feel the victim of
Anyone in particular?
He has friends in offices, offices,
Less friends when they become
Dispensers of patronage.
Does he feel the victim of
The man who has adapted,
Become successful? Yes, he does.
Has he adapted? Not enough, at his age.

IV

Fatigued, fatigued is Don Senilio.
No longer can he summon elegance
To whisper, 'You too, valetudinarian'.
The clear and saffron *coucher de soleil*

Is lacking which could silhouette
Calligraphy of leaves in skeleton.
He shuffles at the bus-stop in the fog,
His feet begin to hurt, and he resents
The unattractive others in the queue.

V

Senilio's regime can not afford
Whipping by Venetian whores.
He has to suffer at cut prices.
Aches of decrepitude
Suffice him. Sweats and twinges,
Toothache, eyeache, hungover
Late haste to work, short breath,
Fear of the reaching crab.
He keeps spry, the old boy, considering.

VI

Senilio is stirred by curves of neatly
Trousered girls. But hair-styles bother him.
Mountainous, maybe, not, alas, of Bath.
Sometimes he thinks 'Rats' Nest', sometimes 'String'.
Sometimes, from tops of buses,
He awards marks for nubility
From a possible total of twenty
Instead of doing the crossword.
He regards the young with lechery and dislike.

VII

Sitting with bad companions in a stews
Senilio observed a veteran fall
Drunk in the fireplace. In stupid malice
He guessed, 'There goes poor Senilissimo.'
It was indeed that potent senior
Whose poems Senilio asked for as school prize,
And asks forgiveness of his gracious shade,
Envies his final slim volume.
Timor Mortis Conturbat Senilio.

VIII

The cigarettes are smoking Don Senilio.
He keeps on coughing.

The alcohol is drinking Don Senilio.
His memory's going.
He re-reads twenty pages of a novel
He knew he wasn't enjoying.
Paper piles up, piles up.
He has had to change to bi-focals,
Wakes at three every morning.

IX

It isn't work Senilio resents
But going to work,
Still having to go to work.
We're all slaves here and some are ageing.
It takes him longer fumbling coins for fare.
The old gentleman should be granted
Chauffeur, scottish rugs, silver flask:
He'd bear down on the zebra crossings,
Cackling as ushers scuttled.

X

Don Senilio
Tips the parking meter
A full half sovereign.
Outside the Turkish Baths
A constable salutes.
He's awarded the Prix Lamartine,
A Beethameer Fellowship,
And a Life Peerage.
Such seedy goods will keep him.

XI

It doesn't do to laugh at Don Senilio
Unless he laughs first.
He's in the business for laughs himself
And likes to calculate applause.
You mustn't think him Doctor Bartolo.
He steals looks out of mirrors,
Adjusts veined cheeks, grey hairs,
And chooses a few words.
He'll time the laughs himself.

Senilio's Distraction Song

And patient monsters in the queue
(The world can't last. I am too mad)
Shuffle aboard the same bus too
Sit paired in seats, the sad and sad
I'd boil them down to the same glue
(The world won't last as I am mad).

Here's absinthe. You'd best booze it too
(The world can't last for I'm too mad)
Illumination could flash blue
To show what hopes are never had
And I might say a thing or two
(Before world ends. But I'm too mad).

Fair morning throws a milder hue
(Too late. Won't last. And I'm too mad)·
On people looking decent too
But I'm not going to say I'm glad
Too late for me's too late for you
(And world must end now. I'm too mad.)

Senilio's Broadcast Script

Riposte to Peter Porter

Good evening. You know my voice. Instructions, now.
Section leaders will break open Cabinet P. *Cabinet P.*,
And distribute the jade-green capsules...Now...

Are you sitting comfortably? Then listen.
Here is music engineered
For this precise occasion. It will last
Eleven minutes nine point four three seconds.
Relax and listen with smiles, employing
Breathing rhythm Delta Ten One Three,
With, if possible, the modifications
In the last supplement. Now...

106

Repeat final cadence
at end of poem

That's better isn't it? But listen again
O listeners sitting contented listen again
It's grave news now I'll pump into your shelters.
The end of the world
Has been postponed. (*Repeat and scream.*) HAS BEEN POSTPONED.

Note: the music was specially composed by Anthony Burgess.

Senilio Re-reads Baudelaire

More reminiscences than if I was ninety...

Great ugly desk, each groaning drawer a year
Stuffed with bits of paper, crammed
With bills, bank statements, songsheets, tax demands,
Keepsakes for what, and letters never sent,
Scraps cut from the *New Statesman*, 1947:
My private secrets are more numerous –
The inside of my head's a catacomb,
Sad slaughterhouse, an Inca pyramid,
More corpses than Mortlake.

I'm a graveyard the moon hates as she shines on it,
Worms drag themselves all through and over it,
Eating and eating again my most dear dead.
I'm somebody's old drawing-room
Full of furniture about to become antique –
You could call it Betjemanesque –
There's a smell of lavender or lilies
-of-the-valley, is it? Anyway it smells.

There's nothing longer than the shortest day
Yearlong of frost and fog, traditional –
One doesn't want to know. The messy street
Extends a boredom to eternity –
Write off living. Come to life
At sunset only, down along the houses –
It's sunset. O.K. sunset, O.K. sunset...

Senilio Remembers his Grandfather

Wide pale pink grey-bristled bald-headed face
My father's father. He frightened me so much
I can hardly remember having seen him often.
His rages were terrible, his woman folk scuttled about
Except in his last illness, bloated bulk in bed:
My father used to shave him with a cut-throat razor.
He would suck his boiled sweets, then put them back in the jar,
Mean old sod. I blame him for
My father's keeping timid and respectable,
My aunts staying spinsters –
And only recently discovered what he did –
I'd vague ideas he went to sea but no, –
A gentleman's gentleman, sometimes a butler
Who drank. When he got hold of money he drank,
Was often sacked. My grandmother's wages kept them.
(I got all this out of my father, in his mild cups.)

Hail, drunken grand-dad! I like a thieving butler.
Your pale head looms leering out of your livery.
I saw an Officers' Mess cook once
Spit in a steak and kidney pie before he put the pastry on.

Senilio Passes, Singing

Solomon Grundy
Bored on Tuesday
Manic on Wednesday
Panic on Thursday
Drunk on Friday
Hung over Saturday
Slept all Sunday
Back to work Monday –
That's the life
For Solomon Grundy.

Words for Senilio to Work into a Patter-Song

'My body is a broad and blossoming meadow.'
VIVIAN DE SOLA PINTO

I

My body is a relief map in eruption
Wrinkles wrinkles wrinkles riddle the landscape
Pimples keep on erecting and detumescing all the time
My face swells and subsides and always finishes older
I have one or two grey hairs among the hairs around my testicles
I give my eyeballs everyday marks for yellowness and bloodshotness
I blow my nose hard each morning to find out how deaf I am
My handkerchiefs are filled with snot
When I make love I do it fiercely several nights in a row
As if it were the last time each time
Then go on the booze for a fortnight
Insulting my dear wife with silences

II

When I wake at four in the morning
There are always two landscapes inside
One is the mess one has made of one's human life
(I can say it only in dreams
I am always trapped in the leaking submarine, the executioner taps
     on the door
I am always back at school or in the army
Having lost my rifle not read Beowulf)
Two is the gurgling and splashing and undermining in the bowels
The snuffle in the bronchi and the sinuses
Orchestrating with bloody birds and aeroplanes outside
Cancer has captured this town and that town one says

III

One gets up makes tea
Discusses the possible public image with the shaving-mirror
Trims the beard sharp

One walks into the sunlight rehearsing wisecracks

One's wife will, mercifully, give one breakfast
Consents to gossip.

Senilio's Weather Saw

If Church spire be clër
Twill be däamp round here

If it be not
Twill be bloody hot

When thee caänt see spire
Church be on fire

And we'll hang the parson, squire
And the whole bleeding choir.

It Is the Blight Man Was Born For

I
Don't knock the door. She's not at home
To chat of Crabbe's or Cowper's verse –
Miss Austen's got the curse again,
This time, worse.

Strides over the moors
A recalcitrant Amazon –
Emily Brontë
With the jam-rags on.

Tears are replaced by
Crimson confetti –
Goblins get hold of
Christina Rossetti.

Poor girls,
I bleed for you.

II
Not given a classical treatment
By any English poet –
Not even Shakespeare.

Whose needling bloodied Duncan,
Sulks lost Actium,
Temper cast out Lear?

Senilio and the Moon

1 *Running Mad*

1

The moon is having her revenges
Inventing girls like the moon.

A sharp blade
Sails the sky.

I saw her through glass, through glass –
No cancelling that out.

What is it that I have
To repent of or relent?

2

I was stammering like a pundit.
At the back of the room appeared

A girl,
Clear and radiant,

Piercing. I glanced. Stammered again.
She went on shining, quietly.

II *Senilio to Christine*

'Ah! Ch-r-r-istine!'
Thus Louis Jouvet with his fine rolling of R's
In the film *Carnet de Bal*
Thirty years ago.
I was a boy when I saw it,
And now I say to you, 'Ah, Christine!'

'Dans le vieux parc solitaire et glacé' –
Jouvet in the same film

Reciting Verlaine.
I would like to walk with you
In an old worn park
With fingers entwined

Chastely, nostalgically

III *Double Sonnet to Somebody Else*

1.	2.
If	It
you	would
were	not
Lady	need
Macbeth	any
I	additional
would	witches.
murder	The
Duncan,	Queen's
Banquo	crown
and	you
all	have
Macduff's	already.
children	Bitch!

IV *To the Same*

Madamina:
You treated me like a dog.
Condemned to some machine
With whirring blades
Mincing to dog-meat. To be tinned.

It was true. I was cut into
Gobbets. How they flew!
But I'm back now, not tinned,
An old dog with
Intelligent eyes.

V *Another Letter to the Moon*

Your re-appearance
New as Laura
Restored my sanity

How refreshing a cup
Of water, cool friendship
And how flattering

With Primavera stockings
And a talent for verse.

VI *P.S.: (Haiku)*

Moon, I too
Can spell:
C, h, r, i, s, t, i, n, e...

Mr Hobsbaum's Monday Evening Meeting

Tradition's fine-meshed sieve will sift
Each man's re-gurgitated toad.
The thin pulse of the word must drift
Up the vague tides of Edgware Road.

They jostle in the crowded room
Severely, not to be out-done
In rich Antipodean gloom
By Mrs Porter's favourite son.

Below the ceiling, guardian of the Grail
The ghost of Dr Leavis floats.
A trim breeze stirs the fragile sails
Of Lucie-Smith's expensive boats.

'Another spider!' groan the flies,
And stagger down the autumnal grove:
The honest gardener's mouse-bound eyes
Protest that he decays for love.

Poems condemned must lose their bowels:
Knit brows acclaim the execution –
Expressive consonants, rich vowels
By ladies trained in elocution.

A slow breeze stirs a beard Lear-sized
(Edward not King) to stringent rage:
'Not in the poem! It's not realised!
An abstract statement on the page!'

[1956]

With a Presentation Copy of Verses

How nice to know Mr MacBeth,
That Harlequin glinter and frisker!
What a gay air of 'I'm Colonel Death!'
Sets twitching each end of his whisker.

His appearance is feline and elegant.
He is certain of each fact he states.
His spectacles prove he's intelligent.
His degree is a good one (in Greats).

May the verse-form remove my remarks
A little bit higher than platitude;
Though we're off after different Snarks,
Accept this book, George, with my gratitude.

Hemingway, Jimmy Bond, and D'Annunzio
Are not in my line and you know it –
You would surely have been Papal Nuncio
If you were not (hélas) a good poet.

May History's mischievous glass
Not show us out of our decades,
With me primly holding the pass,
And you at the barricades.

It Was a Violent Time

'... literary history; it is savage with gang-warfare.'
A. ALVAREZ

1

Who scarred the editor and smashed his snitch?
Which X-bard flashed a chiv, and which one wailed?

Who snapped whose umbrella, then
Tore down urinals, roaring?

Who told whose mistress, in waltz-time
He was out to get him?

Which megalomaniac said, aggrieved,
'You'rr the pushingest mon in poetrry today'?

Who needled whom
Into hurling a glass of water?

Who bashed up Pakistanis in the street?

2

Learn skills. Either the skill of a boxer
And afford to be firm and forgiving

Or deploy your sharp remarks
From a barricade of horn-rimmed spectacles –

That way you win your action for assault:
And when you stab, stab always in the back.

And pray for an unfailing hunch
To know which pundit to take out to lunch.

Jacket it winsomely in primrose yellow!
Here A, B, C are drained of words they said –
Decently wild now, each a handsome fellow,
With X, and Y, and charming little Z.

Footnote to Enright's 'Apocalypse'

Cultivated Signals types
During the campaign in Italy

Used to tune sets in
To German stations:

'The Nazis do Beethoven beautifully.'
And one American boasted

He'd caught *Freischütz* complete –
Thus diminishing his boredom.

(Our chief culture-martyr
Was Glenn Miller.)

The Tedeschi certainly bought
Their magic bullets.

What have we bought?
What have we paid for?

Couples

Three couples in this bar, at different tables,
Two old, one young: the partners are like each other.
One has vegetable faces, chunky respectable
Carrot or parsnip faces: they look fed up,
Keep still, have company manners on:
In private this breaks down, one hopes, suspects,
In rootish laughter, wrinkled grins.
The second is restless and furtive and tatty,
Two mangey carnivores pacing one cage grey-pelted,
He fidgets pipe, taps chin, her fingers flutter
Round the gin she isn't drinking:
They talk and talk, unsatisfied.
The third couple is young, unworried, in good health –
Skin, hair, teeth gleam like advertisements –
They carry off their clothes as elegance –
Speak in a lively manner, gesture like film-stars –
For a few years now are privileged, boss-class.

The girl, a bit plain beneath the glitter,
Glances round at the others,
Is troubled, briefly troubled,
Intelligent under her hair-do.

Anecdote

November afternoon, misty at half-past three,
Chrysanthemums still bright in slant of sun,
And two small girls chattering along the pavement.
The smaller said 'It was shepherds.' The larger, 'I know,'
'Praise him, praise him.' The other said 'No,
It was shepherds.' At last it came to them
And they sang through a verse in wobbling unison:
>   *The king of love my shepherd is*
>   *And he that doth me feed...'*
Having accomplished this they shook off their Sunday School
    smugness,
And trotted away like little animals.

There was the mist getting close, getting closer.
There was the sun, an acid slant of yellow.
It had been warm and now was chill.
Most uncomfortable weather.

Dialogue

CORBIÈRE:

The song of self-praise goes on, too long, too long.
You'll have to sober up soon, old comrade,
And live an ordinary boring day through.
I died of TB at a foolishly early age –
Why do you have to act so finicking hypochondriac?

BELL:

You never had to live with so much praise
In pounds and shillings and pence.
They riddle my vitals, painfully.
It is not true that I am not in pain –
You damned unlucky *maudit* poet, you

And writing so well, blast you.

Ponge: Tree-Trunk

Since Winter's just about to put us on our mettle,
Let's show willing for the Wood's good offices.

Mad bells set off by less than nothing,
Outgoings at our expense, stop now, leaves
Whose whim can cover us or leave us stripped –
The trouble you cost to keep on imagining you
Already only just believable!

Unfasten, fall from me, too honest bark,
Fall to your mates at my feet, from other centuries,
Dead faces of dead masks, committee of husks
To accuse me of your fate, be witnesses –
All of them like you, moment-feeling skin
Which now we see by wet and soil undone.
You are my most intimate virtue,
But die as you must, in the usual way,
Die deliberately, debunk unhappy fate.

And thus the tree is quick beneath its bark
Sharpening the profile death will make perfect.

Whistling a Sober Little Tune: Sunday Lunchtime
(for Edward Lucie-Smith)

GOD IS this
very tiny insect moving
automatic as it were and clockwork slowly
over Hart Crane's page.
Would I have noticed IT
on, say, the *Sunday Times*
which hasn't these wide margins?
I would like to care for IT
but what can one do for an insect?

Practical help is practical only
where appropriate.
Try without hysteria to avoid if
possible killing IT,
except when one is sure IT is a killer.

Pensées for Blaise

1   God is
          a deep breath
          a vote of confidence
          a final stoic gesture

      One must be awake in Nirvana
          or it's no good.

2   Marx would not have said
          religion
          is the opium of the people
      Unless
          he was desperate for something like opium.

3   I lack D.H. Lawrence's
          desperate belief
          in his own vitality

      It killed him in the end too.

4   Of all the religious temperaments
      I find Hart Crane the most sympathetic
      But do not intend to drown myself
      Even in drink.

5   I'm still alone
          after writing all this:
          God hasn't spoken,

      alone and frightened
          I will find some distraction.

6   Je vais me raser
          and put on a tie, turn
          the corners of my mouth down
          like Charles.

      Pride, devilish pride.

Axioms
(for Titus Oates)

1
The brain sharpens its politics.
The personality falls apart.

2
'Good' and 'Will'.
When I will good I am willing my will.

3
Power is plaudits
And various sleazy appurtenances.

4
I won't try to persuade these people.
They would end by liking me.

5
I don't like these people.
They would cheapen my ideas.

Pets
(for Anthony and Lyn Burgess)

1
Domestication for use
At first. Took time,
Could be difficult.
'A good man with animals'
Still commands a price
Like a good garage mechanic.

Provided fleece
Fattened for slaughter
Provided milk
Fattened for slaughter
Provided for transport
Fattened for slaughter

Provided meat, provided meat
Red steak, brown crackling

And some hunted others
Foxes, rats, mice, and such small deer
Got the run of the house

Some castrated
Some kept for breeding
Some fed in winter
Inside the hut for warmth

2
Fetiches elegant profiles
On cave walls
Worshipped killed eaten
Before suburban brick spread

Tamed totems in flats and gardens
Pussies and bow-wows
Mabel Lucie Atwill
Georgian poets

129

E

The idea of the sacred
Has lost class –
A castrated one
Plump and decorative

Writhing on a gate-post.
Fierceness one can fumble.

3

My four kittens are being cute on the carpet
They know where their piss-box is, they'd better

I could have drowned the lot
Before their mother's triumphant birth-purr was finished

I could seize a kitten
Dash out its brains on the tiles

I can get them
Neutered or spaded

But I pick them up, stroke them
Play with them like babies

They play with each other
Stalk scratch bite

I let them climb all over me.
I hope I can give them away.

4

Most of my cats
Came to unlucky ends.

Pinto, made silly by air-raids
Had to be put down.

Jezebel was put down too.
The landlord wouldn't stand kittens.
I hope her descendants are still about
Being a nuisance.
I still feel sick about it.

Heroic Rochester, lean tom
Could leap through inches at the top of the window –
Dragged to the edge of the house and died
With his red guts hanging out.
Three days later we found him, after
Calling 'Rochester, Rochester, Rochester.'
I could kill whoever killed him.

     5
One identifies and feels
A general sense of doom,
Bombs and lung cancer.
(I hope I can give them away to good homes.)

A nuisance all over every room,
'An object for children to learn benevolence from.'
One watches where one puts one's foot.

At present my manners are
                              wreathing and leaping and
Purring for raw liver.

Obsequies for Senilio

My persona has drained, has drained, is frittered away
My shadow shambles, shabby in the street
Only outdoors I meet my shadow, with a stoop
Stumbling past, reflected in shop-windows

Shopkeepers give me good service for my good manners
Give me good measure as they judge that I am poor
Decrepit and respectable

I mocked the coming of old age and now it's age mocks me
I knew about loss from reading and now I know the reality
And loss includes cruel loss of livelihood

> *With serving still*
> *This have I won.*
> *For my goodwill*
> *To be undone...*

My shadow is kindly even to children
(Me, who'd have had the Big Black Wolf
Gobble the noisy little bastards up regardless)
                              What makes it worse
The dogs are barking. Dog barks bounce down every street
Right through the dog-shit. Hark, hark,
The dog at the corner barks at other dogs at other corners;
I order immediate extermination of all dogs,
Old ladies' darlings slavering, panting, rabid muzzles
Eager eyes and welcoming wagging –
Also for execution, ice-cream vendors
Softly, softly murderers of tunes cut off.
I never want to hear 'Greensleeves' through again.

No more this music. A new theme will emerge. I hope.

Let a cat be king of every fence and post.

Old hangers-on are patronising but not with money,
They clap me on the back.
                              How are you getting on?
You're looking well. Keep it up. Take care. Good luck.

Piss off, parasites!

                Gossip greedily mutters
He used to write. She left him.
He's finished now. He couldn't keep off the drink.
How wrong can you get, Chums?

Where are my pride and my panache? My plumes and my presence?
My poet's arrogant look? Not far away...Listen...

    A poet is a proud man
    Implacable his stride
    His lechery and boozing
    Fade away, beside his pride

    A poet is a blow-lamp
    His eyes scorch the veneer
    On bureaucratic furnishings
    And leave a lasting sneer

    A poet's a revengeful man
    Avoid his curse
    Insult him and he'll kill you
    With stiletto or with verse

    A poet is a careless man
    They try to keep him down
    With flattery and with alcohol
    Make him a licensed clown

    A poet will take money
    Not regard it as a bribe
    But maintenance for vigilance
    On the language of the tribe

    A poet is a courteous man
    But it won't hurt you to know it
    The company he likes to keep
    Is ladies and fellow-poets

(A hundred smart in Timon and in Balaam)

I must repeat. Senilio is dead. He was useful while he lasted.
They gave the old boy a decent send-off
With hearses loaded with empty bottles –
Beer bottles, wine bottles, whisky, rum, and vodka, and even cider
    bottles.
The 'NO' of Dada (not the ex-Camberley one) was negated by a new
    truth.
Once again I exorcise the neo-Dada called Pop. *Mors stupebat...*

Muse, forgive my hesitation.
You'll have to put in double time as Anima.
This room (bed-sitting) is walled with menacing books.
My head is crowded with verse and varying cadence.
The dictionary is full of words.

This will be a story in chiaroscuro
Of poetry in prose and verse
And prose of explanation, narrative and gossip.
I hope for help from some of your Frenchmen, Goddess,
And in particular, Pierre Reverdy –
To reach tentacularly down to hidden roots,
Convolvulously strangle ranker weeds.
May my dreams be not reductive but perspective.

Senilio Again

The physical expeditions of an old man
Are formidable (all those ants)
Through the wind
Or up and down stairs

And be careful
Watch his dreams

*

His dreams will be
Sexually ambitious
Watch out watch out
Young ladies
You might be stripped and raped
Or beaten, very pleasantly

*

Mon Dieu, can I stand all this
I don't intend to dive from the end of the ship
Or in front of a motor-car
Or off a bridge
But watch it

*

Goddess, Queen, calm
Moving through the sky with dignity
Preserve me
Winking like I do

Miaou from Senilio

Dundreary, Foppington. Algernon, Wooster
parade the Portobello Road
in cast-off finery:
                (abandoned by Mounties
when a touring company flopped *Rose Marie*
in the middle of Alberta? Brought back
at vast expense?)

Their cheese-mite whiskers crawl into a moss.
They have this creeping Jesus hair-style.

They have these fine pretensions of themselves
pretending to be yobbos.
                    (And Nelson Eddy's dead.)

From The City of Dreadful Something

They have perpetual winter here in Leeds,
So that they can talk about football all the year round.
So we have rain one day, snow the next, and sleet and fog the next day,
And wind all the time.
The first eleven and second eleven
And third and fourth and fifth elevens
Compete for imaginary cups
Cricket they play
In a gigantic greenhouse of bullet-proof glass

Manager Don Revie says
'The weather is OK but the boys were tired.'

***

Not Revie but
        Reverdy
                For Leeds
                Fragmented
Uphill
        People one does not see
Pointed dust
                Whirled
                Mica glints
Grey sun shattered
                Glaring
                Multi-storey
                Car-park
                Vacant
Beetle shards
                Acryline
                Clutter the streets
Vowels cemented flat

***

(Tin Opener)

The refuse-van
        Made pregnant by
                The dust-bin man
Jammed

Caesarean tactics
      Disclosed
         A tiny mayor

      Raging

      ***

To V.G. on his return from the country

What smokey vista the late trav'ller meets
In drear perspective, LEEDS pressed out in streets!
The railway lines along the hillsides must
Committee a brute blue-print through the dust:
Glossy, in howling wind, the photo shocks –
LEEDS, multi-technic, towers or squats in blocks...

      ***

each	every	bread
single	van	and
limousine	means	circuses
in	at	
the	least	
car–	a	
park	mile	
implies	of	
one	experimental	
administrator	film	

      ***

Mani in the Merrion Centre

Hell is one great big daylong and nightlong compulsory ambisexual
      gangbang

Hell is a poetry reading packed into the Albert Hall where you sit
and know that sooner or later every single member of the
audience, *including* X and Y and Z, is going to get up and
read his or her poem, except when the Cup Final is being
played in the Interval
Hell is a new brute building called Polytechnic full of hard slab
stairs and peeling walls and low ceilings and handles that
come off and there is particularly noise drilling banging
grinding throbbing that follows you from room to room
always in the room immediately above the ceiling
Hell is a shithouse scrawled with graffiti that have never heard of
wit fingered in shit and floors strewn with soiled toilet
paper and newspaper and gentlemen have not lifted the
seat and you dare not emerge because of heavy guffaws
and horseplay heard outside
Hell is a committee-meeting where sociologists are talking sociology
In Hell there is nothing to read by the underground press and oh!
that scabby typeface and ah! those pockmarked photo-
graphs of beards and all that sprawling artnouveau
Hell includes also the Merrion Centre with its special subways for
mugging.

***

'Hell, dear sir, is what I say it is.
Hell is you, my friend, when I am in that mood.
Why, Leeds is Hell, nor am I out of it.
Why, I am Hell, nor is Leeds out of it.'

For Good Wednesday
(after putting up with Good Friday and Easter Monday)

I offer pediments, pulpits, peppermints and parapets
Also balconies and ballrooms –
All the architecture I would offer you,
Except for grim staircases and lifts
In pseudo-tall sky-scrapers in Yorkshire,
My least favourite county
— I was invited to a reading in Morecambe
And there's a train leaves Leeds at about 4pm
And climbs over the Pennines,
And climbing down the further side
One feels oneself once more in England,
Green fields and stone walls and sheep,
And not in this glaring dirty pseudo-Scandinavia
Where people have horrible accents
Except art students, who do not eat people.

To David Broomfield*

Greetings from London, my dear David,
I hope your health is much less rabid
For this term's symbol is the frightening
Of a fine-nerved steed by lightning –
I've purchased, from the National Gallery,
The Géricault version, on *my* salary!
Also expended, *par ma foi*
50p on Delacroix –
Meanwhile here's Lord B., rather fat,
In Turkish drag and funny hat,
Who, if he'd been a bit less sinister
'd have finished up as our Prime Minister,
Which would have meant things going gaily
And not like Gladstone and Disraeli.
Thank God this P.C.'s small, my powers
Could keep it up like this for hours.

* Written on a postcard of Thomas Phillip's portrait of Lord Byron in
Turkish costume, from the National Portrait Gallery. Sent to David
Broomfield, Department of Art, History and Complementary Studies, Leeds
Polytechnic. [Ed.]

Written in January

Aquarians
February is coming
Let us not wince at
This grim month
When we were born.
We will do better in the summer
Than the rest of them.

Aquarians adapt easily
To blue skies and sunshine
And the sound of water.

Unfortunately
We can't stand bloody Leeds.

Tight-rope Walker
(for Alex Henry, dead)*

Tight and tense and taut as the rope, I. My feet know the way
Better than I do, the rest's sense of balance. The spangled lights' play
Transforms me irridescent, a shimmer-wing insect. The crowd gape
      in their places.
The best bit is when I stop in the middle and spit in their faces.

* Alex Henry died by falling from a high building in
Leeds in the middle of the last decade. [Ed.]

And Welcomes Little Fishes In
(for John Milne)

The crocodile inside
Is very sick
It has interior teeth as well
When given bread and marmalade
It grunts 'uh, uh'
I don't know what it does with all those cigarettes
It swallows long jaw-fulls of whisky down
But as for the swinge-ing horror of its fiery tail
This merely thrashes about in muddy water.
There's a big waste of teeth going on there.
It's left with a grin.

Poem for Günter Grass about Askesis

I'm afraid my cat says,
Speaking from the grass roots,
'Cancel yourself out, friend, cancel
Yourself out.'
How ascetic can you get?
However I shall flatter my cat
Comme d'habitude
By luxurious tickling under the ear.
By the time I've finished with him
He will be purring not talking.

Poem to pay for a pair of shoes

As one gets older
One notices it in one's feet:
'My feet are killing me.'
One dies from the feet upwards.
Hence the importance of shoes.
One crams into elegant shapes
Regardless of corns and calluses
And malformed toes and fallen arches.

Do not show me a painter's self-portrait
Show me his old shoes.
A drawerful of worn-out shoes –
Autobiography.

Variations on Francis Bacon

There are three chairs in a room.
One is irrelevant, it contains a typewriter –
No that's wrong, the typewriter is not irrelevant,
It's a silent reminder that something has to be written.
One of the chairs is completely empty.
The remaining chair contains a man sitting.
He is hunched and terrified. He is on trial for his life.
He dare not look in a mirror, his face would condemn him.
Another scapegoat. *He wants to be Pope.*

Cauchemar

It's a race between me and death
Through all these ugly bastards in the street
People actually hitting each other in the street
With sticks, not crowds but
Two or three people at every corner
Shouting horribly. A muscular man
Is wrenching a muscular woman's arm.

Sudden, a carriage. Overtowering come
Two oriental potentates
In twisted tall flamingo headdresses,
And huge hooked noses, leering.
Thank God, that lot moves off.

Because I do not know what town I'm in
I ask the way to the Public Library.
At the door a gendarme is waiting –
'We were expecting *you*.'
A librarian-like-a-schoolmistress charges me sixteen-and-eightpence
    overdue.

Another copper cautions me
For kicking library doors in and
Throwing books away in the park.
I am not allowed to borrow any more books.
I shrug.

And now here is the Financial News

And when the day's markets closed
They decided that money was wind and excrement
And demanded and drew in all the world's currencies
And put all the bits of paper on one big blazing bonfire
Then they gave every sovereign country a great big refrigerator (or
    ice-box rather for the ice-man cometh)
And every country was allotted its very own vegetable as a unit of
    currency
At the end of the day's trading the American lettuce was flopping
    and flapping droplets of plastic mayonnaise all over the sky
The English radish was limping
Everybody was wearing unwieldy awkward brown necklaces of French
    onions
But kept on complaining about the reek of garlic
The Spanish and Portuguese kept shouting Olé Olive Oil Olé Olive
    Oil Olé Olé Olive Oil (et cetera and if possible et cetera)
The Welsh leek also was limping and wept when somebody shouted
    'Yah Daffodil'
The Germans expanded and blew out and swole their great crimson
    beetroot arse-cheeks
The Scots haggis was limp as a sporran and moreover was ruled out
    as not a real vegetable
The English radish was still limping and also shrinking
Scandinavian turnips parsnips carrots were lumpish and greasy
    because only partly boiled without salt
Chinese rice rose against Japanese rice and Japanese rice rose
    against Chinese rice
Russian vodka was given away buckshee but was also ruled out as
    not a real vegetable
The English radish was very limp indeed
Italian necks got very very long wrapped round and round and round
    with spaghetti (bolognese)
Indian betel nuts were disgusting on the pavement
Africans pelted everybody with misshapen sweet potatoes
So the Irish had to stick to shamrock and very silly they looked with it
The English radish suddenly had an erection and swelled and rose
    (English rose) and erected even more and spread through the
    atmosphere around the globe until the whole globe looked
    like one gigantic radish

The Arabs were missing dates and slowly the poison the whole
    bloodstream filled and the waste remained and killed
(I knew the phoenix was a vegetable and also an oil well)
So the other nations decided to convert to fish and try to think
    decimal and finny
And so on and so and so

Rasputin Messing with the Rose Madder

Everyone agreed that the Mad Monk
Was much too much of a good thing,
So they tried to kill him off in various ways,
Alas, without success.
Even such obvious violence
As shooting and stabbing,
Large draughts of hydrochloric acid –
Even the gas-chamber didn't work,
The stink of sweat and vodka drowned the gas.
He crawled away,
His greasy beard leaving a long smear on the ice.
They stuffed his nostrils with cucumbers –
They tickled the soles of his feet with tinned sardines –
They shaved off his pubic hair and sewed on plastic rose-petals –
They tattooed the Lord's Prayer backwards 9,999,999 times on his
         back
They had him impersonated in a Hollywood Epic
And not even by Vincent Price.
No dice. He still wouldn't die, even from shame.

At length the solution arrived – Brain Washing!
'Rasputin,' they said, 'relax in this machine
With its cushions and its switches and its pretty lights
And the soft soft music and seductive voices
And this will teach you how to go on Doing Your Own Thing
More evilly because much less obtrusive.
And then they'll all say what a charming chap you are,
And so helpful besides.'
                              He couldn't resist it. They
Electronically instructed him All About Art.

So he became one of the most quietly cultured epigoni of Hampstead
And taught students how to teach other students how to teach
         painting
And occasionally exhibited innocuous landscapes.
To compensate his other exhibitionism
They let him flash it once a week at the Tavistock Clinic
Before the eyes of his admiring family.

And if he still felt a compelling need
For something on the side
There were always first or second or third year students
(Girls, of course. He wasn't like that),
Who needed extra encouragement.

Wordsworthian/Ovidian Epistle
to Patricia Highsmith

Miss Highsmith, O Miss Highsmith, Dear Patricia –
No blush would mantle our good Laureate's cheek
For this effrontery, but James's would –
Henry I mean, not the footman. That odious Strether
Is utterly more wretched than poor Ripley!
Poor Tom's a-cold, we'd shelter him,
Make him a retrospective Harvard man,
Warranted Ivy League, the nicest type,
With an instinctive nice discrimination.
Psychopathic, yes, but not psychotic –
Scapegoat for the massive psychic malaise
Of all the (just how many?) vast United
States of half America's north half.
How good a President he would have made
With all of Carter's toothy dishiness,
And Shadow/Nixon, shaved at five o'clock –
You know of course the work of Doctor Jung,
And hypostasis of the *Animus*.
(I've trouble with the *Anima* myself).
Think of Tom Sawyer, somehow self-educated,
And there you'd have him in a Brooks Bros. suit,
But he'd know better than a Brooks Bros. suit.
(I only ran to Moss Bros. suits myself).
If I parade some Limey prejudices
Your lady-writers give me ammunition,
Mesdemoiselles McCarthy and McCullers,
Dorothy Parker, and yourself not least.
So *right*, his palazzo, Venetian,
For me, at least. Not Corvo's. Not Visconti's.
How witty is his choice of lumpish victims!
(The passage in your work that most makes wince
Is when they dub drab Mongibello, 'Mongy'.
I know that coast. Christ halted near there.)

How justified the death of Jonathan
In being awarded an heroic end!
I didn't know that photographs could haunt
On coloured book-jackets. Yours does.

Dark, handsome, noble, Sybilline, compulsive –
Your witch's eyes demand obedience.

I rest my case. Give *me* the daggers.

With fondest

Lament for Bing Crosby

Dead, Mister Crosby, dead
This unbelieving generation
Would smother you in soft white christmases
Molasses of gossamer indulgence
Your greatness, sharp legato greatness
O Mister Crosby, Mister Crosby, Mister Crosby
(I trust that I can make the matter clear)
You were greater far before all that
That going other people's ways down various roads
When you would take it up and keep it going keep it going
With Mercer, Mister Mercer...also dead
No 'entertainer', but an actor, a true histrion
Did you not act with Fields and not upstaged?
Fields, W.C., dead also, long ago in glory
Didn't you ramble with Armstrong, also dead
We've got to áccéntuate the pósitive
Eliminate the negative of smooth Sinatra
I got a message from the Mocking-bird
That Sinatra was dead on his feet
Sinatra made of plaster like our Joanie
Biederbecke taught *you*, in mummer's digs,
Music, disced Debussy and Stravinsky,
And it stuck. You got rhythm but also
Style, like you said   style
There are a few enthusiasts left
Who can tell the difference
Between the first and second versions of
That Old Black Magic   Old Black Magic
Got me in its spell   Gone Fishing
Bob White
              Mister C
                        We're gonna break it up tonight

LETTERS FROM CYPRUS

To the Goddess

A letter
From your own island

So long without a poem
It seems to heed fear

Three frights

First, train from Paris
Got into Van Gogh landscape
I was manic with brush-strokes

But it narrowed
Into a tunnel,
Became dark, pale, dark

And Christine, started coughing
Ghastly in a rising pitch
Her face paled to paper.

Something clicked in my brain
Started shaking, shaking, shaking
Kept on screeching

All the way through the tunnel
Had to be given whisky
Luckily she held me

Secondly, in Marseilles,
I bit deep into a peach, rotten

An insect jumped from the stone
It wasn't singing the Marseillaise
In the gutter where I threw it
Was a chicken's head torn off.

Third,
In Nicosia an elaborate café
With expensive aviaries
(They went down one floor.)

One cage contained
Hundreds of small yellow parrots.

Next door were peacocks
Partridges, other resplendent fowl

(The other side had a small lake
With a large swan.)

There was also a vile black snake
Writhing writhing very quickly

It stabbed at a peacock
Which pecked back sharply.

Part of the show, we assumed
Until the waiter told us it
Shouldn't have been there.

Then it was gone
The snake, vanquished by the birds, one hoped.

Frighten me again but
Not too much
Do not frighten me to death.

Illumination on Mockers

The laughter of the mockers can
often be overheard, but one must
penetrate its disguise. It can seem to
be the barking of dogs, crowing of
cocks, fussiness of motor-cycles.
           Tootings

The mockers wear
good suits. Their teeth are
clean. They sometimes shave their pubic
hair but never in public.

They have motor-cars which give
them continual orgasm. Always, always, always.

How does sand get into one's Ouzo?
The mockers secret agents...

They commit the sexual act in
the Sunday supplements.

The things that happen on thick carpets
must not be thought about.

They have amusing wallpaper.

They are the abomination and the
end, including the Whore of Babylon.

My toes are looking senile.

Wish in Heat

I wish I knew a millionaire
With a jet plane
To fly us over to Henekey's
And fly us back again.

Pussy

You were best cat ever
But not good at cleaning.
Lolloped up and down the road,
A bit lame
You crawled from under a car at me
In Talbot Road, W.9,
And then got run over in Leeds.

I had to fetch you in a dirty towel, stiff
Then bury you.

You were a good cat,
Black and white and grubby,
Demanding two meals a day.

Part of Larnaka

Chicks, noises
Like insects

Transistors
Playing pop-music

(Pop music is
Bad)

Dogs are bad
At night

Woof, woof,
Woof, woof, woof

Resounding against
The architecture

Cocks
Will crow and crow

(Cats
Are very discreet

Children,
Not)

Worst is
Motor-cars –

Taxis. Piff – Piff.
I want a machine-gun.

Cyprus Monastery

A long way up
To the top of the mountain

Faith took the taxi
Round those upward bends

(Swedes from UNO
Half an hour in front of us)

White room, white room
For visitors

Black beard, black beard
With a smile for visitors

Black coffee for visitors
And sweets for the children

(Sideways, I thought
'Monks are supposed to make liqueurs')

The church had
Wooden seats for eighteen monks

High round the walls. I didn't
Like the ikons

There was a bit of the Cross concealed
In silver

I pretended to be
Reverent

Quatrain for Christine

And prophilaxis extra to the stars
Plonking on multiple feet
It was tra-li in the extreme
Lumbering vans and mammals
No fifth line.

Clerihews

Guillaume Apollinaire
Was hardly ever there.
His butler was instructed to ask who
Visitors were. Then pass them on to Picasso.

Guillaume Apollinaire
Took off into the air:
'Everybody must know it!
I'm the archetype of the avant-garde poet.'

Cricketing Song

The crickets kept saying 'Coca Cola, Coca Cola'

There is an American general called *Coke*,
And a C.I.A. man called *Coco*
By his friends,
(But he hasn't got any)
There are various television producers
Called Coxes
Nothing to do with the apples.

I prefer brandy
Or Ouzo
Or a nice cup of tea.

Or a pint of bitter,
The bitterer the better.

Cyprus: Noon
(for Redgrove)

Friend,
       foreboding
(Stass is just round the corner)

Sweat like sweat, eyes
Brown aniseed balls, with whites
Like hard-boiled eggs
Chilled under the tap
The shower pricks like
Igloos. It is hot and getting
Hotter. Stay indoors
Darkness presses down an
Oblong blanket. I drink a
Slim goblet of very cold
Water. After that
Alcohol, thin and stronger than gin,
Tasting of aniseed.

Trees rustle outside.
Doves coo noisy
Grapes are heavy.

The cats are evasive,

I too evade myself,
Insubstantial as an icicle
Running with sweat and ouzo.

From Rimbaud on Troodos

...on top of the mountain. A long way
up. Donkeys veer round precipices. They
never fall, but I do. Deep precipices,
ravines of evergreen, over yet another
green drop. Stones, great chiselled
boulders, and labourers humping stone
I could dizzy and impale on
trees, dash a forehead against stones.

Who is this Governor, for a mansion?
(Shopkeepers and booze and fog and gas.)
I am the overseer, gangleader,
foreman, strawboss. My forehead has dried
into wrinkles, gullies where streams of
sweat once ran.

The labourers glint with irony. They
know their slowness is quicker than my
Gallic wit. I swear blasphemies, again.

What am I doing as foreman? I should
be humping stone myself. Or being rich.
Or writing verse. But this has been given up.

It's a long way down, veering. I dread
but grit my teeth. Another bottle of Ouzo,
please for the shakes.
        Aphrodite has left me a grimy dove-feather.

Andiam! Let us be richer, build bridges.
Steel bridges, filagreed.

Please send me the Encyclopaedia Britannica,
Aphrodite! I will read the whole bloody
lot, I swear it.
        Hommages, comme d'habitude, A

The

the
priest
combs
the
lice
out
his
ginger
beard

the schoolmaster
is clean-shaven
wears a blue shirt

both
polish their spectacles

Sleep

Is mostly brown or
(very difficult) grey

If one is drunk it can be
Blue or
Green

I like it pink and cream

For C. in Cyprus

I cannot share your sleep
You are utterly abandoned to it,
Landscaping all over the bed,
Making it rich with your body.

I am left out of all of this
Except for a kind of privilege
Of being present,

Or being bashed by your elbow.

When I'm awake I am alas awake,
Which is a reason for getting drunk.

Over-stimulation

My eyes are weeping
Involuntarily
They ache
I keep commuting
Between my strong glasses
And black glasses
And no glasses
My naked eyes have seen too much
The colours are too bright
Especially the flowers.

The buses go through too much country
So many miles of mountain
So many different trees.

Alcohol helps
I wish I could afford taxis
All the time.

166

Municipal Moor

(Leeds)

Two dogs
Chase across the grass

(Owners
Lark)

Wrinkled bark is
Older than municipal statues

Among the statues
The aldermen

Are more charming than
Queen Victoria

Or the dental caries (sculpture)
On this building.

One white benefactor
With white mutton-chop whiskers

On a white plinth
Against

Rows and ridges of
Red roofs.

Monastery Cats

A very clean building
On the mountain top

With a wide courtyard
There were also all these cats

About fifteen
They kept on running about

At least two tabbies
Two black and white

Various varieties
Of ginger

And black
And white

And one classical
Tortoise-shell

They wouldn't come
If one purred 'Pussy'

But then I found
A lump of Dutch cheese

Which I threw to them in bits
The tortoise-shell came first,

Then I had the whole lot
I felt guilty

Because of two old women
Who might have needed food.

But I needed the cats.

Accident Prone

A tendency
To get oneself bashed up –
Blood on the face,
Black eyes, bruised ribs, etc.
Even burns.

One pretends to have been in a fight
But has only fallen down
Drunk.

Letter to Alcohol

The subtlest flatterer of them all,
Pool of Narcissus –
'Echo, Echo, Echo,'
One belches.
Moreover you taste nice.
Let the hippies keep their hashish,
I am faithful to you

And to somebody else as well
Whose name begins with a C.

One

Every so often up against the edge of
Something horrible. Must be oneself how
Could everything else be so bad? So, one is mad.
Why are there never any ash-trays?
Why can one never find what one is
                              looking for
Although there are clutters of objects
Pushing themselves into one's hands –
                              like dirty socks –
Searched for two days ago,
Now no use.

Why can't they invent a method of shitting
That doesn't leave one feeling unclean?

(They are always researching into
More elegant childbirth,
Tidier abortions.)

Porter said once
'What sort of a wedding gift
Is a red lavatory seat
For a man with piles?'

How can one comb one's hair without
                              a comb?

In Bedroom

On bed

        Discontented wife, covered with
        Dirty sheet,
        Cigarettes and matches, (moved)
        Two horrible orange pillows
        Two tobacco burns   (by me)

On floor

        One empty beer-bottle which
                      contained water.
        Two socks (fairly clean).
        Sand (rather dirty).

On armchair

        One empty cigarette-packet
        One book, open upside-down
        Several letters and telegrams,
        One empty match-box
        One piece of silver paper,
        One piece of cheese.

Recollections of London

A brown velvet-textured
High crowned sweeping-brimmed
Hat
Was walking along the road
In front of the traffic, the buses
In Oxford Street (in Hell)

It was crawling, mole-like, buffeted
In front of the wind
An elderly lady, very brave
Leapt out to rescue from the wheels
Then pushed her way back through the shoppers
Offering it upside down,
As if she were begging

An old gentleman, eventually,
Reclaimed it,
Smiling,
Smiling, apologetic.

London, Again, Dreams

Why
Did you
Have
To get pregnant
By the wife of a Tory M.P?
It
Will have to be carried
Down the main aisle of Westminster Abbey
By Mr Speaker –
Then interred in the dome of St Paul's.

Along Westbourne Grove taxis will be wailing
and everyone in Portobello Road will be
                          buying Boy Scout uniforms,
And Girl Guide whistles.

They will actually clean the streets
And all Irishmen acquire BBC accents

Antique furniture will be given away free,
Or for a few cigarette coupons.

Musak will be banned
Will be banned
Will be banned.

Juke-boxes will be banned.

One-armed bandits will be banned.

Irish barmen will have to take a literary test.

Or so it seems

Stass's Pictures

1

Are very rich
Almost too rich

Full of colours
Particularly green

And pink and blue
And beige and orange

The episodes
Are poignant

About
Men and women

Sad and somehow
Joyful. Very sad.
And fertile.

2 *Adam and Eve*

This must be after the Fall.

They are wondering what to do
When they have to leave the Garden.

Adam has a calculating cocky
Slant to his eyes –
Also lecherous and genially defiant
(Thinking of horticulture)
Like his green moustaches
And green fig-leaf.

Eve appears submissive.
But there is a certain smugness
In her well balanced stance –
A fit of the sulks (humility)
And a sensual gratification
She knows she has got her man

And all around them the Garden
They must leave soon,
Where there are oranges and pink
Tree-trunks and doves
Fluttering in pattern
Nevertheless they are experts
At growing gardens
And child-bearing.

3

Slain heroes
Dead in green and red
Mourned over
By weeping women and
Eucalyptus carob olive trees
And vines
And brown and white mountains

The landscape is alive
With colour
Neighbour.

Kyrenia

We took buses
To Kyrenia

The road was blocked
From Nicosia

So went forty-five miles
Out of the way.

We called on Roy Jenkins
At his hotel

But he had left
That morning

(We wanted him
to cash a cheque)

On the way back
An Enormous

Orange sun
Reproached us

We got back
Before the wine-shop was closed.

Pyromaniac

Suddenly he was amazed by
This fresh packet of Swan Vestas –
Tore
The sides out as instructed.
Each scarlet bulb
Will pay for a flame

Safety matches are
Drier and more discreet
Hurrah for
Bryant and Mays

Work out the average number of matches
For
Yourself. There might be a prize.

But if you want a bomb
And don't mind burning your hand
Explode a fresh box
Of Swan.

Dear Peter

As you are the worst Jonah I know I address
this letter to you.

(Remember the time at Victoria
We boarded a train for Dulwich
And landed in the middle of Kent?
They said it was a signalman's mistake,
But was it?
And George arrived late in Leeds for a reading
And the porter had put him
On the wrong train.
At first I heard and believed
'Porter put me on the wrong train.'

Why does one always expect you to arrive
Half an hour late? However –)

We crept down the stairs from your flat,
Walked along swinging Queensway
To Bayswater Station very cold and early
Then Victoria – pushed through the people,
Collected luggage, pushed on with heavy luggage,
Until Stass's Gurdjieff moustache
Bristled among the crowds, smiling
And his children were jumping up and down,
And Mary was smiling patiently
And we joined the party, then a hitch –
A dark emissary from the Travel Agency
Saying my cheque was made out incorrectly
– Actually the advance had been bounced
By my former bank-manager (I dropped him)
So I had to do a complicated business
Of changing cheques with Stass.
I here insert a parenthesis –

Dear Peter, I am very annoyed.
With some bank managers.
I exempt the Walham Green Westminster.
Whenever politicians get slightly
Constipated, they
Call it inflation, and
Take it out on us, saying
'Credit Squeeze',
I know where I'd squeeze them if
I was in power.
We should be in Zürich playing chess –
Or organise a bridge team
With Genghis Khan South
And Tamburlaine North
We've been too damned decent.
We are the clever ones (vraiement).
Why
Aren't we rich?

Train Dover gentle crossing train
To Paris. Fields of sunflowers in
Interesting oblong patterns, wheeling. Then
Paris! The journey across France cost us –
Four adults four children
Fifteen pounds devalued sterling
For ice creams, coffees, beers, and fruit.
Nothing to eat.
Of course the Parisians seemed to us pinched and mean.
Another parenthesis called
(ILLUMINATION

The depths of one's disillusionments! Paris was
the imaginary capital of the empire
of the intellect. Beirut and Rome are
splendid cities: I know a good city when
I see one. London abides our question, but
Venice has no motor-cars.
But Paris! Such shabbiness. So much
money for two beers!
Show me Vienna now, mate.)

***

For Stass

Slain heroes
Dead in green and red
Mourned over
By weeping women and
Eucalyptus carob olive trees
And vines
And mountains brown and white.
The landscape is alive
With colour,
Neighbour.

*

Moi, je suis anglais
BUT
The English in Cyprus
Avoid each other
Justifiably

Whoever had more
Circumscribed
Manners of living abroad
Than the English?

Lines of Wimbledon
Or Aldershot houses
Built for them alone
In streets not roads.

The Officers'
Mess
Or the Sergeants'
Mess

An architectural mess
Here I sing the Internationale

Non-Mediterranean Life
(for Odysseus Elytis)

You don't know half of it
Always the sun and love trees and sea
All acceptable clichés
In a very good climate

We (English, hélas) have a poor climate
Up, down, cold, or warm or wet
Sometimes uncomfortably foggy.
One doesn't know what clothes to put on.
It's generally wet and dark. I hate it.

You would weep at some of the
Architectural additions to these towns.
Eclectic?
H'm...(Ask.....)

One chooses one's places
Comme d'habitude
And this is not fascist.

'In the endless boredom of the plain'

In the endless
Boredom of the plain
The ambiguous snow
Shines like sand

The copper sky
With no light
The moon lives
And dies

Oaks like clouds
Fade
In their processions
In forests

Copper sky again
With no light
The moon
Repeats her performance

Dirty crow
And mangy dogs
What will happen to you
When the weather gets nasty?

The bloody boredom of the plain again.

Letter to President Johnson

The thing I am fed up with, with the United States
Is that I am getting fed up with the United States
It used to be a religion with me
Even more powerful than the Soviet Union.
Uncle Joe killed that one.
But I am prepared to reconsider.

I will be
Prepared
To reconsider
My anarchical
And basic
Cynicism and pessimism
If you will back
Barbara Castle
As the next Prime Minister
Of the Hallowed Isle
Where we happen to live.

Letter to W.H. Auden

Dear Mr Auden
          as Judy Garland said to Mr Gable
this is a fan letter
          and for once, hélas,
you cannot ask good John to shut the door
moreover
          hélas
I have got used to writing
          what looks like *vers libre*
having caught
          this habit
          not repeat NOT
from those pseudo-avant-garde
          black
mountain freaks
          but from translating
Pierre Reverdy
          whose work you maybe wouldn't like
him being a Frog
          (he has indeed
a quiet elegance of dignified
          confrontation and alarm)
it has also distressed me
          to hear it rumoured
that you consider French the language of hell
(but isn't music brandy for the damned?)
and did you not claim once
    'While to his left upon the bench,
    Muttering that terror is not French
    Frowns the young *Rimbaud* guilt demands,
    The adolescent with red hands,
    Skilful, intolerant and quick,
    Who strangled an old rhetoric.'

Wallace Stevens Welcomes Doctor Jung into Heaven

'Doggone, they've let you in at last, Doc! Gee,
I'm real *glad*.' And indicated angels puffing horns
Rococo with praise and bray and bray,
And proffered to him saffron ice cream cones
Topped up with glacé cherries and chopped cashew nuts.
'Ach! Horn of Plenty,' the good Doctor said.

Translating Reverdy

Agonising re-
               Appraisal
               Of words
Turns of speech
               One thought one knew
That dreadful 'On'
               How
Can one avoid 'One'
               Although
One can say 'we' occasionally
Or even 'you'
Or switch the whole thing to the passive voice
And what the hell are those inverted commas doing
When other punctuation marks are gone
                    Including
Question marks
               As for the imperfect tense
And what to do about reflexive verbs
               It perhaps reassures itself
               That something is always
               Doing itself in
Never, in English, 'tu'
OK, Pierre, mate, but

Manifesto

I.	II.
Poetry is made of words but	Un coup de des
Concrete Poetry is made of	
CON	N'abolira
C R	JAMAIS
E TE	La syntaxe

Autumnal for Reverdy

Ragged dahlias
               In the very heavy
               Archaic vase
Are waning
           Skeletal
Outside
           Gross privet leans
Beyond
           The mist persists

'Peret, assist me'

Peret, assist me
with propellors and steam radio
and advertisements recommending
Colman's Mustard as aphrodisiac
and Bovril for clearing the mucus of the brain
Wither new show business into old infamy
with its clouds of purple smoke
call up the whole tribe of cats
inspect the stripes and claws and whiskers
and sound the alarm for attack
on throats stuffed with sawdust
and plush lozenges
and celluloid consonants
and rhubarb punctuation
and one hundred and seventy-nine Sumerian proverbs
each blatantly untrue
plus the usual lead piping rubber tubing
    drain pipes filthy old tobacco pipes archaic
    female contraceptive devices and the
    dentures of Elizabeth, Bloody Mary, Mary Queen
    of Scots, Hannah More and Anne of Cleves
    (why should she be left out?)

Hutchinson's Collected Haiku

1

The table aches with
Emptiness. What is missing?
Ach! The typewriter.

2

The mills are silent,
The looms no longer click. Nor
Does my typewriter.

3

My typewriter? Why
Not? I was the only ba-
Stard to get near it.

4

What sod, what hairy
Barbarian from the foothills
Raped the typewriter?

5

I dreamed I heard a
Metallic scream. I turned over.
I am bowed in shame.

6

I will get Sandle
For this, for this foul outrage.
I will scrag Sandle.

7

Whitbread, Lord, hear my
Not undeserving plea. Get
Back my typewriter.

8

No handmaid with green
Eyelashes and nails can boast
Typewriter's beauty.

9

I mourn. I cover
My head with ashes, hear me,
Typewriter come home.

10

Like Orpheus I go
Lamenting into every
Office. Heartbroken.

11

'Oh! Oh! Oh! Oh! Oh!
'Oh! Oh! Oh! Oh! Oh! Oh! Oh!
'Oh! Oh! Oh! Oh! (Dies).

For Pearse Hutchinson

People are hanged for many a crime.
I always wake up just at opening time.

Poem of Congratulation

All human births are incarnations.
Always there are angels in attendance.
The father must be for a time, like Joseph, a drudge,
Cleaning the house and carrying flowers.
I throw in this herb for good luck.

Marine Easter Poem for Wendy

Whales, teethed sharks, electric eels
All the powerful fish
Attend, and also
All the respectable fish
Cod plaice haddock
Be there with
All the little fish
Sardines, whitebait, goldfish and
Everything that swims in bowls
And all the varieties of the excellent
Herring, including kippers, even in cellophane
Attend and also even though in tins
Tuna and pink salmon
One always needs a porpoise although
We haven't got to the magic bit yet
The pageant is assembling
Shellfish, crustaceans, molluscs
Oysters, limpets, whelks
Mussels, winkles, crayfish, octopuses
Shrimps and prawns (Norwegian)
(There's a lobster close behind me)
For some reason they are bringing up
For you only
A large scallop shell to balance
Attended by mackerel and cupids
And be gently breezed to shore at Paphos.

Refinding Ruth's Umbrella

I find it invigorates
(So to anthologise)
To find it again
And an excuse to apologise

And to recover
Without any thorn
This blunt instrument
Among the alien corn

And what an effort
Among cleaning up
This mess – to find it
And then cheering up.

And so to find it
Among all these voices
Makes the heart wither
And also rejoices.

Through material objects
Are messages sent
Your umbrella and this pen
Divine instruments

'Why, Mr Lancaster'

Why, Mr Lancaster,
Mr Lancaster, my dear Lancast -er
I find your letter gay
(*Old* meaning) in an entertaining way
But the meaning just a little bit obscure.

I always told you it was *Mauberley*
NOT Moberly – she
Was that interesting don
Who went with Miss Jourdain
To meet Marie Antoinette in Versaill -ee.

If there's something I resent
In the letter that you've sent
It's the horrible insinuation I
Have anything owing
To that obscene Leonard Cohen –
Guitars are *painted*, not played, blue as sky.

I cannot keep this Gallaher and Sheehan
Patter up any longer, so
Revert to *vers libre* – or
Is it syllabics? I don't know.
But any anthology
Partially kills somebody
Who isn't put in, but
He can get into some other anthology
With enough persistent talent.
True, I was defending
My rights as a one-poem-man
Against Donald Davie's strictures
Which struck me as hysterical
And as he picked on poor Patten
Somebody had to defend him

(Being *in* anthologies also kills
Particularly in M. Horovitz's).
You still seem to be making
Some moral point that escapes me –
Perhaps you will elucidate?
            With best wishes,
            Martin Bell.

Question

Which is the correct leg
of a bishop?

The right leg
Has blue buttons down the gaiter

The left leg
Is, of course, scarlet

Zip-fasteners
Are something between turquoise
                        and amethyst

Read these runes
Whoever can

And camp out on the proceeds.

To My Watch

Little ant, busy, busy,
Why tick on when I'm not interested?
Better to leap about
Like the white cat in the garden.

Given to Jannice

Max Ernst, Max Ernst
Lend me thy green mare
Down along et cetera
And we will go to some bloody fair
Slinking anonymously
And name-dropping
Prodigiously

For Horn Obbligato by Jeff Nuttall

A landscape for the gentry
Picture postcard for the poor
The ghost of André Breton
Is beating on the door

A chaise-longue for the whizz-kids
Poxed entrails on the floor
The ghost of André Breton
Is beating on the door

Salvador Dali collars
Cash, Avida Dollars
The ghost of André Breton
Is beating on the door

Neo-Dada complements
The Colour Supplements
The ghost of André Breton
Is beating on the door

The Albert Hall was open
For Bollocks to be spoken
The ghost of André Breton
Is beating at the door

It is not illegal
To consult Hegel
The ghost of André Breton
Is hammering at the door

For Peter Redgrove

Poets. What an awful word.
Language a bit posh.
Like a bow-tie well-managed.
A butterfly in the collar.

No need
To talk of zip-fasteners.

Reading a 1914-1918 Anthology

And it is nasty still to call them queer
Who wouldn't stay wounded, would rejoin their mates
In trenches. And abandoned all their dears
Who kept on knitting, knitting just like Fates.

Poet and Society

Spy, Marlowe, cobbler's son – he saw them
As bosses he could puppet and exploit.
He blew them up the better to condemn them.
He loved his monsters. Jonson saw the point.

Magnates, creeps, pushers: forced to move
In competition, made his talent cope:
A brilliant dwarf whom they could hate or love,
Subscribe to in bound volumes: Mr Pope.

Pity, bored pity, throwaway wincing
From streets, shops, houses which he couldn't hate;
He said love failed him to be more convincing –
Our Larkin, laureate of the welfare state.

Yet our statistical showbusiness age demands
Something. Rebellion? Let the preachers
Be expert, non-beat. 'The adolescent with red hands'
(Auden on Rimbaud). Not comprehensive teachers,
Or poetry and jazz. Not all that stuff.
Perhaps we shouldn't teach them. Enough is enough.

For Pasolini's Friend

You sado-masochistic sod
Pretending to be Son of God
It would not be at all our loss
If you descended from the cross,
And, supposing you are You
Gave us a miracle or two.
Unless you send us a sure sign
We'll have to change the Party Line.

'MacGregor swore an oath'

MacGregor swore an oath
Against the Art department.
He'd walk into their land
And teach them just what Art meant.

Horses can be allowed
If kept in tidy stables,
But the Railway Age is better,
For that brought in timetables.

So always keep it presto,
And never, never lento.
You can talk about the *early*
But not *late* Quattrocento.

(Tune: *Anything Goes*)

Yeats was almost
        with it once before
Recommending
        Rabindranath Tagore
Now God knows
Zulfikar Ghose

Then there came the
        even palmier days
Stephen Spender
        pushing Dom Moraes
Now he knows
Zulfikar Ghose

        Got get at it to-day
        Be fanatic to-day
        Asiatic to-day
        Très, très syllabic to-day
        It's traumatic to-day
        You had better obey
                Who knows?

Bandsmen all please
        hurry on the wagon
B.S. Johnson's
        pouring out the flagon
Of his prose
There Zulfi goes.

Loyal Address

Your majesty your image
Confronts me on this
       ten shilling note
You do not seem glad
       to be there –
(It must be a responsibility
guaranteeing all that money.)
You are not comfortable
You hold your head up
Like a young lady
       finished in a
       finishing school.
Encumbered with jewels
You have survived
       Crawfie, Racine,
       and the A.T.S.
(I hope they taught
you how to enjoy Racine.)
One can only say
Good Luck.
I am a republican,
although that
would be more

Queens were luckier
When their heads might
Have been cut off
Your neck is elegant.

Killing Flies

This massacre is partly
Like the affair on St Valentine's Day:
In that version I am Edward G.
But also
        this Perfumed Fly-Killer
Makes me Jahveh
            judging the damned.
Bluebottle flies are damned, are damned,
          are damned.
Their gross bodies make their souls deformed,
There is no possibility of Grace.
Only this last one I pursue
Flapping pathetically about
Can go to Purgatory. But
St Bluebottle is impossible. He would buzz.

Writer's Block

A jewelled piece of furniture of hell,
This block. An elaborate machine
Of twisting gleaming parts
Hewn from the solid metal. Try
Your teeth on that.

New Litanies

Because I know that I shall turn again
Pray, please, Paul Éluard
Because I know I will be bored again
Pray for us, Baudelaire
Because I know I'll spit in spite again
Sharpen my tongue, Mr Pope
And let me take with it a little more water
Mr Cole Porter
Because I am a vieux *marcheur*
Stumbling up the flighty stairs
MM Laforgue and Corbière
(And to hell with Yves Bonnefoy).

From purgatory, Auden, where you must be
I pray for you,
Kindly reciprocate
(And we'll hang the Golden Fleece upon a sour apple tree)
And take that grin off your face, Max Jacob.

Against Lies

It is not true – I am free
From all this Xtian stuff –
One is still in the nineteen-twenties
When occasionally an aeroplane
Would punctuate
Extraordinarily
Various dull clouds
One still agrees with H.G.
Wells, Bernard Shaw, André
Breton, Picasso, Aragon, Éluard,
All that lot. Even André Gide,
Who slinks in, in the last line.

Inertia (Spleen)

Our faces, hopeless,
Melting like blancmange
Tell their own story.

Numbness soars
Over the campus
Hands,
Ten idiot fingers
Playing shadows behind churches.

Nevertheless
When you smile
The street is flooded.
What goldsmith did you employ
To set the trees as gems?

Here
Coldness and spleen are married.
O.K., the ship will arrive
At noon precisely.
I will get a big hug
From my big brother
At twelve o'clock.

About Sociology

I have, God help us, taught the eleven-plus.
By the headmaster's secret instructions
Between four fifteen and four thirty I
Taught intelligence tests.

I have heard well-salaried bourgeois parents
Offering to pay for evening instruction
Or threatening to complain to the head.

I have seen the complacent faces of Inspectors of Education.

I have seen rebellious hairy students
Drop out and drop back into themselves
Looking for a barber before
Answering advertisements and filling in forms of application.

I have heard plump nail-filed charge-nurses
With motorcars and mortgages
Endlessly urging recalcitrant alcoholics
To lower their sights
And be content to conform to the norm.

I have heard a greasy bossy nurse
Screeching like a school teacher
Nagging and threatening old men and old women
As if they were backward infants.

Ode to Education

I represent
      the teachers
      and the teachers
      and the teachers

I would like to teach
      something and
      something and
      something –

I have something to communicate
I should not have to walk up
      and down flights of stairs
Looking for pupils.

Don't they know they have something to learn?

We do not need headmasters
Standing up for the Beatles
And washing their front windows
In their own urine.

Something to be taught –
Possibly "tradition"?
At any rate, good manners.

Victory of the Yobbos

They will come from television
On several sides.
The secondary modern yobbos
The grammar school yobbos
The public school yobbos
The engineering yobbos and
The scientists.
They were not always yobbos
They were condemned as infants
To mass media –
Jesus wept, parents
Competition, competition, competition,
Fighting, fighting fighting

Always a boost for stupidity
Always more money for

Successful salesmanships
Exploitation of the stupid.
Always money for show-business yobbos
One almost prefers
The anarchist fuzzy-wuzzies.

Solitude Is Everywhere

Pathways wind among gathered harvests
With the self-assurance of things that are going to last.
If I trample along roads and streets close only
To the threshold of suffering and death

In wind's curls and children's curls there's
Too much sun that isn't for anybody
And everywhere there are curls of a weight
Like fruit freshly cut

Green

Here are fruits and flowers and
                leaves and twigs
And here is my heart too
                which only beats for you.
Don't tear it up with your
                two white hands,
Let your shining eyes
                accepts it as a present.

I'm turning still
                covered with dew
Which this beastly wind
                has frozen on my forehead.
Let my tiredness, lying
                at your feet,
Dream of a few minutes
                which will let it rest.

Pour L'Élection

His true Penelope was
The elder Dumas. (Homage
Nonetheless to *Traviata*).

Poets like being
Musketeers,
But each wants to be Aramis.

Kafka has it somewhere,
So many messengers
And so few kings.

Reference to Thurber

This is how
Three poets talk:
'Touché!'
'Touché!'
'Touché!'

'There was a bloody-minded poet'

There was a bloody-minded poet
Who did not like his blood at all.
So, more completely not to know it,
He filled his veins with alcohol.

H

Poem for the National Westminster

My profile at full length
                 of melancholy
        Corrodes a moping silhouette
            Right through my cheque-book

They will use it to prototype
              Special cheques for students

Instead of Mickey Mouse

Pissing

It is, alas, a pleasure
A full schooner
Of precious liquid
Like *The Fighting Temeraire*
Or *The Wreck of the Deutschland*
Rescue all those bloody nuns.

Please re-apply on the dotted line

Paper handkerchiefs are
So convenient, carry them,
Big Chiefs,
Between ham sandwiches in
Pockets, handbags, school satchel
Cat-baskets, wigwams –
Wrapped up in pages of
A second-hand paperback
Convenient from stalls.

You might find some rotten with snot
Yellow in pockets
Of a military uniform.

And take a bus afterwards,
Put them in with your ticket
In the French Letter Pocket.

You could even smoke them,
Between clean dry cigarette-papers.

Innocent Fencing

Wrought-iron fence
Wrought-iron fence
Who am I
To give offence?

*

Apart from the fact that
Reptilian rococo curves
Deserve more offences
Than anything I can do deserves.

*

It isn't even rococo:
More like Art Nouveau
Which is the silliest fashion
Which has ever been taken back into fashion.

*

I do not like
Iron fences. Especially
With silly ornamental curves,
Inside themselves. Cruelly.

*

'New styles of architecture, a change of heart.'
(Quote)
Where are these new styles, then?
All these office blocks? Heh?

Do something.
Apart from
Librettos.

Incidentally in praise of Barbara Castle

My cat was stiff with rigor
I covered his fur with a cloth
Smelling of floor polish
And carried him home like a baby
Through the street
Carrying a dead cat on a Sunday morning
With neighbours peering through the curtains
The grave we dug in the garden
Was a little too narrow
We had to force him in
Poor Pussy
A cat and a half
And a half.
May drunken careless motorists
Beware
I hate them
And will persecute them

Fragment of Eggshell

To the movement of the Egmont Overture
They urged me into the supermarket
To interview the manager
And break as many eggs as possible –
'We must break into his Ego.
You can't make an omelette without breaking OMs.'

About Bombs

My mild father
                    enjoys swearing,
The sound it makes.
                              He couldn't use
Theology or/
                    sexuality
Because of his mother and my mother.
Instead of
                    Damn or
                              Fuck
He used to say BLAST
Quite often
                    before the War.
Tra-la, la-la, la -aa
Tra-LA, la-la, la -aaa
Oh *bother* the flowers of spring.

Alter Ego

Impossibility of communication

I stamp slowly in my gaunt
Grey stubble, my tall bones
Up and down the bar, embarrassing
People
                    Grimacing with my glass of bitter
I stop at the mirror
Muttering
'I want to go to Hell with the long-haired ladies
I look for Hell in the mirror
Eurydice'

The Maenads

Of course in my very next dream
After reading in Jung about Wotan
I had to encounter the Maenads
And of course the Maenads' leader
Turned out to be my very dearest
I wasn't exactly torn to pieces
Except by jealousy
Among those she'd seduced
Were some of my favourite pupil-sons
And one of her Lesbian friends
Attacked me with her claws but I escaped
The Gang of course included when unmasked
Almost all the girls I'd ever known
A, B, C, D, E et cetera
And my ex-wife and my best friends' ex-wives
Vampires, vampires all
Naturally of course orgy developed
Bottles broken, tables overturned
And frenzied dancing started
I wouldn't dance, I said, quoting Astaire
Not neat enough for me, not feat enough
And then they formed into a human chain
Which turned into a spiral rising, serpentine
But I pronounced with great authority
'The décor is by Gustav Klimt'
Standing aside, stage-managing
I proved myself the biggest bitch of all

Dream

I was instructing a painter
About a painting I had in mind.
It was to be naturalistic, like Magritte.
It was to be based on David's 'Death of Marat'.
But instead of Marat in the bath
There was to be a daffodil (*sic*).
The daffodil was lounging peacefully
In the warm water, all along its length,
With a neck slightly warped by the warmth
And a head above water at a slightly unusual angle
And the water folded over like an eiderdown.
I was almost beginning to draw it myself
In my impatience.
I saw the shape of the bath, and the floor, and the corner
of the room.

Will You

Despite
Your puritanism

Allow me
Friendly access

To all your
Interesting landscapes?

(I will not tell
John Knox).

You know I
Love you.

To Exorcise Baba Yaga

Shrunken family festival
Album page of postage stamps
Walls of fathers, brothers, aunts
Grandparents, granddaughters, daughters
Sisters-in-law with Ph.Ds
Photographs flashing irony
On spider and shiftless son

Pots, plant-pots, flowerpots, plaster busts
Crammed on to every shelf
Brass, ivory, china, varnished wood
Steeped and soaked, unvaried mood
Shining in gall and no regrets

Her voice rauks on and on
Every familiar anecdote
They were wrong and she is right
Useless to try to edge
In a redeeming doubt
She brandishes her deafness

She glares and quivers pathos
I swallow my spume of rancour

The screen blares Eye Tee Vee
I cringe behind my book

Creep out of bed in the small hours
To live an hour alone, read, write

I need the aid of a nimble, thin, black cat

To Spite Baba Yaga

This revealed truth has come to me after having on each of
two successive days, spent a whole hour
without taking my eyes from the Mandala
I have now called Tiresias

My life has been suspended in a cruel balance,
tugged by cruel pulleys in two opposite ways,
which means a paralysis of the will at crucial moments.

To spite Baba Yaga

For what withholding from an infant
I do not remember, but that infant
has repeatedly taken revenge. Cutting off
his nose to spite his face.

To spite Baba Yaga

A weak male spouse and a dominant woman
is the classical way to produce a homo-
sexual son. But not if the woman herself
has an obvious flaw. Then it is possible to defy.

To spite Baba Yaga

To be constipated then incontinent.
To be miserly, & prodigal
To be a clumsy, cowardly, bullied boy,
despised by his compeers.

To spite Baba Yaga

To still be cleverer than those stupid bullies,
To refuse to jump in, in the Public Baths,
and then, by himself, to conquer
the sea, learn to swim.

To spite Baba Yaga

To succeed in two examinations,
and then fail to be First in the
third. (A Poet's Third.)

                                             To spite Baba Yaga

To join the Communist Party,
sell the *Daily Worker* on
his parents' doorstep, carry
a poster down the High Street.

                                             To spite Baba Yaga

After three years,
sending a cruel
telegram, to abandon his first
sweetheart and comrade.

                                             To spite Baba Yaga

To join the Army, hastily, in
the wrong corps, to get
away from home.

                                             To spite Baba Yaga

In the Army, to be self-consciously
a Good Soldier Švejk. And
to get away with it.

                                             To spite Baba Yaga

To reach final contempt for Stalin because he sat
down with Churchill, that
raddled Britannia, that
Pantomime Dame.

                                             To spite Baba Yaga

Après la guerre finie, to take
the first job offered, to get
away from home again

                                             To spite Baba Yaga

To make an unwanted marriage
and rudely refuse to allow
his parents at the civil ceremony.
(Yet the fruit thereof was fair.)

                                    To spite Baba Yaga

To persist in school-teaching,
although a despised occupation,
yet in a manner slovenly without
conscience. Supreme self-torture.

                                    To spite Baba Yaga

To drink oneself almost to the dogs,
yet take the difficult turn back.

                                    To spite Baba Yaga

In the short run now, all my library
books overdue, awkwardly short of
money from overspending, my
work neglected for two months.

                                    To spite Baba Yaga

The new moon began my salvation
twenty odd years ago.
The thorn now possibly at last removed.

'Assez connu. Les arrêts de la vie. – Ô Rumeurs et Visions!
Départ dans l'affection et le bruit neufs.'
Deflores, remain by my side. And to you A.,
mon enfant, ma soeur, vows renewed.

(Let Baba warn the ladies,
You'll find out soon or later,
That good or bad,
Most men are mad,
All they say or do is the-atre.)

220

Private Seasonal Greetings

Although you're still alive
Your ghost is here.
This furniture, these books,
You haunt.

*

If clothes sprawl on the floor
Heaped like a shapeless sea,
If the whole sink-full's unwashed,
Not my fault, but your ghost's.

*

Footsteps, just outside
But your ghost won't come in
To see your photograph
Still on the mantelpiece.

*

Enjoy your Christmas Day.
Your ghost too
Has turkey-piled plate
And brandy by the neck.

*

And in bright morning sun
By pub half-way down Church Street,
I wish you Happy Xmas, dear
In 1967.

*

For C.

There are several other places
Apart from Florence and Rome
And Venice
And Beirut and Tripoli
(The two latter messed up by Americans)
I would like to take you.
One is Brighton
The other is Glyndebourne
(I have a special dispensation
There about having to wear evening-dress)
There are certain operas I would
Like you attend in particular
One is *Marriage of Figaro*
Another *Der Rosenkavalier*
The list could be extended.

This is just a letter.
                              Martin.

p.s. I would also like to go to Aberdeen.
Newcastle is O.K.

A New Leaf in a Diary: For C.

My mother's concern, fanatical,
converted me against
polished clean surfaces, exact
temperature of oven
et cetera. (Gracious living is a
tyranny. Glossy and hot with hate.)

(O.K. I know about mothers
having nothing else to do with their spare time
and not enough money to spend it on)

Whenever I saw a home I wanted to trample all over it
in muddy boots with studs. Even spurs.

Now I'm concerned, however vaguely,
with walls and ceilings and floors
comparative prices of vegetables
times of meals and whether dustbins get emptied
Et cetera.

(Love is the figure that makes a pattern a pattern,
brushes the hair to a pattern.)

Let us amaze ourselves, then, with
paint and carpets and hoovers and washing-machines
even holidays.
Jesus wept, I once thought, bleeding holidays.
Now just holidays, straight.
You have gentled me into this.

(Uncouth as I am. Still. Gentled. And not castrated).

Tra-la. If you like. Tra-la.

For C., with, I suppose, gratitude
or This is a love poem

No matter howsoever many times
He or she may say 'No more'
At last they meet again and wonder
Finding themselves fit into the same landscape
Say for an instant 'Why ever part?'
Sharing an instant the same eyes

(Landscape of hospital beds and bottles and nurses
Landscape of grasping bars bottles and uncouth barmen
Landscape of washing-up reproaches unmade beds)

Always she has trains to catch
For iron necessities, career
Or ethics, is it? Or disgust...

Willing to admit his wit, his reading, his intelligence
His varied confusion of experience,
Almost a cracker-barrel sage. But no respect for a poet.
Beneath the surface she thinks poets
An overrated lot.
                    Although she causes poems,
And will again. With her looks and talent
And sympathy. An unwilling Muse. Write soon.

Poem

How nice to have known Mr Bell,
In a very short spell of his life.
Although life may have been hell,
At least you were known as his wife.

He had a good gift for vernacular,
His irony's very complex,
Though physically not très spectacular,
He thinks a great deal about sex.

Alcoholic, but also a poet,
On the rack, on the rack, on the rack,
(There's a rhyme here, but you do not know it),
Have him back, have him back, have him back.

Although it's not safe for to plan it,
And see to the money between,
And it's difficult to make verse scan it,
Return, come again, O Christine.

Dream/Letter/Poem for Christine

Daughter and mother, wife, mistress: Muse: 'regina of the clouds':
(There's a bit of the original Swinburne left in all male poets) :
(The English, lacking dandies, produced Max Beerbohm,
Who did the dirt on the bards.) : (*this aside*
Is dedicated with irony to Edward Lucie-
Smith. Look, no hands and my mask isn't slipping
Yet. But just you wait. However...)
Irony is self-protective and masks are strip-tease –
Sweetest Christine, do not be fooled by my fooling,
Apply your physical grace and your strength and your intelligence
Your tenderness and skill and bitchy intuition and also
Your superreal beauty, focus your brown eyes
On our dilemmas. Look, there is this dream...
It will have to wait till I've filled in the background detail –
Why do I come dripping in my hair from sleep at 02.30 hours
At the end of a hard week?
Work for others but mostly for myself –
Tape recording a narrative for Will Barton
And persuading him to indent it as verse,
Three exhausting mornings – helping Wendy
To re-write a poem about an epileptic mackerel –
And I hope I have got three of Lyn's poems into the *TLS* –
Then evenings
          and Friday
              Saturday
                  who is on the stairs
Why has the procession stopped outside
              those shadows are shaking themselves
again
      qu'est-ce qu'on va faire
      typing   translated Pierre Reverdy
                      mostly
      with a typewriter rubber.
one relaxes   (The trouble, Pierre,
      after indenting and indenting
Into this slack, shall one say, quasi-hexameter base.)

I was pleased with my version of 'Other Jockeys, Alcoholics',
And went off to watch television.
                              Part of two programmes
Something upset me
Broke off. Could do nothing more. Went to bed. Slept.
Woke up swarming with this dream. Hence this pen.
Sitting on the side of my bed with a coffee-cup.
(By the way, one of the reasons 'Other Jockeys' pleased me
Was that it reminded me of Redgrove,
Masculine friendships are easy if one is not queer,
No need to touch. But with women it's dodgy.)
Well, then, this dream. It was overtly sexual.
Luckily none of my fetishes seems to have emerged,
Unless I've already repressed them. A lot of the detail's gone.
It was about the first girl I was in love with, J.J.S.
In a confusion of meals and cinemas, in a mixed crowd of people.
And trams. It seems I won her. To congratulations.
'We always knew you would.' We undressed.
We embraced although there was no penetration.
She was beautiful. I was proud. But it ended.
In a vagueness of loss and rejection and vain seeking.
I awoke without an erection but full of trouble.
One of the troubles was that even in the dream I knew
That today she would be fifty-four like I am.
I should perhaps have married her. I think she loved me
As I loved her. But both of us were stiff with inhibition.
(There was no male rival to provoke me. Only a girl friend.
I have always suspected girl friends' girl friends,
Especially when they are plain, suggesting butch cups of cocoa.)
And so I betrayed her with D. who was two years older than I was
And so would be fifty-six. A fellow Party Member. She was much
        shorter than I am.
She had been a year in France and was experienced.
Not me though. We fumbled for two years.
There was no penetration. We were both sick roses.
We were almost married but the war came
And preserved my demi-virginity until I was twenty-eight.
The rest you know most of. Back to the dream.

Latent content: the clues were on the television. 1. A "comic" sketch of two old decrepits courting like geriatric patients. 2. A "comic" sketch about a man who kept a wife in a bed in the sky at the end of a kite-string. He swapped wives with another man similarly placed, by swapping strings. I never thought Harry Secombe would remind me of Reg Varney. 3. Secombe said he liked appearing with Lulu because she made him look tall. She replied he made her feel thin. When I first saw him in an army show he was as thin as a leaf, and his style was as taut as a kite-string. Now he sang a sentimental song with all the oiliness of Burton doing his Dylan Thomas bit. 4. Then a film. Sophia Loren, whom you alas resemble, was married to Anthony Perkins, as thin as a leaf, but wanted to leave him because he was still an irresponsible small boy, a Peter Pan.

All too near the knuckle. I tried to type again but could not revise.
I glanced in the mirror and was fat and fatigued and elderly. Abruptly
     I went to bed.
Cocteau says that in every artist is a woman and the woman is hateful.
(Being a queer he didn't think a woman could be a real artist).
Some say that all women are one woman. Some, surely, more equal
     than others.
But you are my Muse, forever, whether you like it or not.

29/12/77 Didactic Poem

Sleeper, demi-sleeper,
(For you are so cunning)
Sprawled on your bed/litter/couch,
At floor level
(Surprising what one picks up at floor level)
With a red quilt
Operatically spread
And darker blanket
Operatically spread further –
What news from your objective psyche?
Are the thwarted archetypes stirring
Out of their fairy dark forest?
Very little clue
As you twist and toss
Operatically asleep
And make a further spreading
Over the bedclothes, operatic,
Of a mane of dark hair.

'Behind despair'

Behind despair is forlorn hope.
Inside the sinking heart
It cherishes a place to mope
Though ordered to depart.

A Bad Day in the Bedsitter
(to the shade of Thomas Hood)

Where to find the poem for a bloody day like this?
Cup after strong cup of tea and then upstairs to piss,
Too damned idle otherwise to drag myself from my seat,
With far too many books and not quite enough to eat.

Nightmare had nudged into waking its nagging disquiet
And kept my nerves shaking with panicky rumours of riot.
The postman went by the house without leaving a letter.
It took a good few cigarettes to make me feel better.

Odd passages of verse and prose consumed but no pattern
Emerging to any purpose. I sat and sat on
With no inspiration, listening in vain for the doorbell.
Boredom turned my friendly room into a quiet corner of hell.

Then my blank poise is shattered by afternoon noise
When the school pours into the street all the horrible small girls and
    boys,
And the clatter and banging and screeching are starting the dogs off –
I'll go mad, run out howling, and ripping my togs off.

Remembrance of things past is sad in my situation –
Where are my girl friends and old friends and witty conversation?
Not enough P for a pint, which makes things a bit worse,
Just enough energy left to jangle a few lines of verse.

May this next night bring dreams according to the good Doctor's
    prescription,
Prospective not reductive to the imagination.
I'll get up early and calm and wash out a few pairs of socks,
And some kind of letter, not O.H.M.S., will come through the box.

A Vocation Possibly

This tiny room, this cabin, this monk's cell
Pantaloon decrepit scholar's den
Shuffles me like a full pack of cards
(One has to be firm and extricate the Jokers)
Although there's hardly any room
Between tall Wardrobe, piles of Bookcase
Great Raft of Bed in the middle, almost unmade
Narrow corridors to squeeze sideways
Past Chair, Armchair, Wardrobe, Table, Sink
The books refuse decorum on their shelves
But leap into heaps on to table, chest of drawers, bed
Or sprawl face downwards open on the floor
Among footprinted newspapers, crosswords half filled in
Then on the shelf between clock, cotton-reels, postcards, scissors
The villanous small transistor wafts me
A ridge of high-low pressure, round and round and round
(For five whole weeks I was mad Robert Schumann
Until I said Thank God, Thank God for Ludwig Van)
The typewriter gnashes angry silent teeth
I almost forgot dead matches, crumbs on the rug
It's safest in the armchair in front of the electric fire
Regarding the Mandala and then the Sacred Cat
Reading or better writing without falling asleep
(I'm afraid to sleep at the moment for dreams are refusing to come)
I almost forgot the coiling, creased and soiling clothes
Wreathing into a snake-pit
Suggesting I go out or at least get washed
But No, No, someone is playing me
Laying me out as Patience
Generally the game known as Demon
That comes out only once in fifty-seven times
I wish I knew what card I really was
The Jack of Hearts, Dame Pique the Queen of Spades
Or else the Curse of Scotland

'To start to shift uphill'

To start to shift uphill such load,
Sisyphus, needs your extra effort,
Indeed, one needs one for the road,
Art is long and time is short.

Already on its modest way
Towards the crematorium,
My heart, regardless of display,
Beats like a muffled drum.

'And here I am still'

And here I am still
And even older
With all my anxieties on
And the stink of old corruption

All is still in print
And still reprinting
Glaring headlines
Ribbons of old fears

Index of titles and first lines